1687

1789

The Story

1838

# of Southern

1861

Presbyterians

1865

1887

T. WATSON STREET

1930

John Knox Press / Richmond, Virginia

1961

Library of Congress Catalog Card Number: 60-11623

Second printing 1961

© Marshall C. Dendy 1960
Printed in the United States of America
7822(20)D.3237

Foreword

The Centennial Committee of the Presbyterian Church in the U.S., with the approval of the General Assembly, authorized the writing of two books apropos this historic occasion. One of these was to be a history of the Presbyterian Church in the United States and the other a consideration of its role in the world to-morrow. The committee commissioned for these tasks two men it felt to be peculiarly fitted for them. We are happy now to present this history by T. Watson Street as the first of these volumes.

It is our firm conviction that an honest look at our Church's history will teach us both to rejoice in its accomplishments and to ascribe them in humility to God, to confess its mistakes and to renew our confidence in His readiness to use it, to understand it better and to love it more. It is our hope that the present volume will render this service not only in the Centennial year but also through many years to come.

While this volume carries the imprimatur of the Centennial Committee, the author was encouraged to write in complete freedom, and his views, therefore, do not necessarily reflect those of the Committee.

JOHN NEWTON THOMAS, *Chairman*
Committee on Special Literature

Preface

This book was written at the request of the Centennial Committee. Much of the Southern Presbyterian story had to be omitted and almost all of the material had to be presented with the greatest brevity, due to limitations placed on the length of the book. Appreciation is expressed to the Centennial Committee for the assignment, and to John Knox Press for aid given. I am indebted to Rev. Ben R. Lacy, Jr., Rev. James A. Millard, Jr., Rev. William Childs Robinson, and Rev. John Spragens, who read the manuscript and made suggestions; to Rev. Norman Dow, librarian of Austin Presbyterian Seminary, for his help and that of his staff; to Mrs. Wright Hallfrisch for overseeing much of the secretarial work. Most of all I am indebted to my wife, Sara Crews Street, for interest and encouragement, in addition to great help in preparing the manuscript for the publisher.

T. WATSON STREET

Contents

		PAGE
1687-1789		
CHAPTER I	*The Mother Presbytery*	9
1789-1838		
CHAPTER II	*Growing Pains*	27
1838-1861		
CHAPTER III	*"Our Southern Zion"*	44
1861-1865		
CHAPTER IV	*The Presbyterian Church in the Confederate States*	60
1865-1887		
CHAPTER V	*Desolations Repaired*	75
1887-1930		
CHAPTER VI	*The Church in the New South*	94
1930-1961		
CHAPTER VII	*Changing Climate*	110
CHAPTER VIII	*Conclusion: Heritage and Mission*	125
CHART OF PRESBYTERIAN DIVISIONS		127
BIBLIOGRAPHY		128
ACKNOWLEDGMENTS		130

CHAPTER I

The Mother Presbytery

TOWARD THE END of the year 1755, a group of Presbyterians met in a church in Hanover County, Virginia. Already there had been several events which made this year a memorable one for them. In February one of their number, Samuel Davies, had returned from a trip of fifteen months in England. He had journeyed there to collect funds for the young College of New Jersey (Princeton), established by the Presbyterians, and while there he had won new freedom for those in Virginia who did not worship or minister in the State Church, the Church of England.

In that same month of February the great George Whitefield, most renowned preacher of his day in the English-speaking world, had made his third visit to Virginia and added new force to the great religious revival stirring the Southern colonies. By midsummer General Braddock and his English forces had met a crushing defeat on the western frontier near present-day Pittsburgh, Pennsylvania. The defeat left Virginia open to attack by the Indians and sent a wave of terror through the colony. The terror was reflected in a greater seriousness of life and spread of revival, as well as increased migration of some settlers into western North Carolina. In October the Synod of New York approved the organization of the first presbytery in Virginia.

Thus, on December 3, 1755, four ministers (two others were absent) and three elders held the first meeting of the new presbytery. It was the Presbytery of Hanover, the mother of all Southern presbyteries, covering the area from western Pennsylvania to Georgia, including Virginia, North and South Carolina, and the settled parts of Tennessee and Kentucky. Presbyterianism in the South was beginning its organized existence.

AMERICAN PRESBYTERIANISM BEFORE
HANOVER PRESBYTERY WAS FORMED

This new presbytery was an addition to the growing strength of Presbyterianism in America. Some Presbyterians were gathered in two small Churches of Scottish origin, and some belonged to small Churches of continental origin, but the great majority was gathered in a body that was destined to become the Presbyterian Church in the United States of America. This "American Presbyterian Church" was a young Church. With missionary help from the Presbyterians of England, Scotland, and Ireland, churches had been established, many members of which were Presbyterians who had fled persecution abroad. Out of these churches the first American presbytery had been established in 1706 in Philadelphia, and thus it antedated Hanover Presbytery by about fifty years. Its leader had been Francis Makemie, who cared for groups of Presbyterians in Maryland and eastern Virginia and who was buried in Virginia. Growth was rapid, especially in Pennsylvania, New Jersey, and New York, and in 1716 the Synod of Philadelphia was formed.

In the meetings of this first synod were reflected the hopes and problems of the Presbyterians. What does it mean to be a part of Christ's Church in a new land? What does it mean to be the Presbyterian Church in America? Prayer, thought, and labor were used in large amounts as the Church worked out its course, one step at a time. In 1717 the "Fund for Pious Uses" was established for missionary purposes. Concern for the unity of the Synod created much discussion in the 1720's. How could the Church preserve unity of witness and protect orthodoxy of doctrine without insisting on a dead uniformity? Some ministers and members contended for strict acceptance by ministers of every word, "without any variation or alteration," of the Westminster Confession of Faith. Others favored subscribing to no human document but only to the Bible. The result was the compromise Adopting Act of 1729, which required subscription to the Westminster Confession, but left some room for individual differences if these received the sanction of Presbytery. This principle of freedom within limits has continued to be the basic position of American Presbyterianism with regard to doctrine, though how much freedom and how much limit has often become an issue.

Soon there came the Great Awakening! A tremendous revival swept over the colonies. This revival not only affected the religious life but also became a dynamic factor in the social and political life. Presbyterians were leaders in the Awakening as well as benefactors from it. But alas, revival brought excitement and excitement produced trouble. Two sides formed in the Church. The differences between them proved so great that the "American Presbyterian Church," the Synod of Philadelphia, was divided in 1741. Human and sinful factors played their part, but the two groups, "Old Side" and "New Side," were struggling with great issues: "Whether true spiritual exercises implied . . . great excitement,—whether conversion was a rapid or very gradual work,—whether evidences of grace were decisive, or necessarily obscure,—whether true revivals were attended with great alarms . . . and great distress and strong hopes and fears,—whether a collegiate course of education was a necessary preparation for the ministry . . ."[1] These questions—the nature of conversion, the methods of revival, and proper qualifications for the ministry— were to disturb American Presbyterians many times in their history. As a result of the division there were now two synods. The Old Side, taking the name of the Synod of Philadelphia, opposed many of the methods and much of the doctrine of the revival and was the champion of tradition; the New Side, called the Synod of New York, supported revivals and placed great emphasis on religious experience. These two groups, though divided, constituted the mainstream of American Presbyterianism and were to be reunited in 1758.

In the midst of this revival excitement the Presbytery of Hanover was born, formed by the evangelistic New Side Synod of New York. Thus the new presbytery was not an independent organization but part of the mainstream of American Presbyterianism. It was the product of the concern of the Synod of New

York for the spread of the Church in the South. The minutes of this synod, as well as those of the Old Side Synod of Philadelphia, record the "unwearied application" of the Presbyterians in Virginia for services, and the urgent attempts by the two synods and their presbyteries to share the few available ministers.

PREVIOUS EFFORTS TO ESTABLISH PRESBYTERIANISM IN THE SOUTH

The organization of this mother presbytery had taken place only after decades of labor and prayer in the South, much of which had at times appeared to bear no fruit. Presbyterians from France, seeking relief from persecution and war in their native land, had made settlements in Florida and South Carolina as early as 1562, but were soon overcome by the Spanish. In Virginia there were Presbyterians, including some among the early settlers of Jamestown, but the lack of religious liberty led them to migrate to Maryland about 1650. French and Scotch Presbyterians had established congregations in South Carolina about 1687, and since that time Presbyterianism has been continuous in that area. The earliest presbytery in the South was organized around Charleston before 1722. It did not become the presbytery that was to be the agent for the spread of Presbyterianism through the Southern states, since the area was still only sparsely settled and ministers had to be secured from Scotland. There were also Scottish merchants and farmers in the coast towns of Virginia and North Carolina who sought to secure ministers for small groups of Presbyterians. Also in the 1680's there was a new opportunity in Virginia when the Presbytery of Laggan of the Irish Presbyterian Church sent out missionaries. Among these was Francis Makemie, the father of American Presbyterianism, who came to Virginia in 1684 and devoted some of his missionary labors to Presbyterian groups in the eastern part of the state. But because Virginia had a State Church, Presbyterianism did not take root and no lasting congregations resulted. It was not until itinerating missionaries were sent out by American Presbyterians of New

Jersey, New York, Pennsylvania, and Delaware that Presbyterianism in the South was to gain permanency with strength. That missionary activity was begun as early as 1719.

Missionary preaching led to the new Presbytery of Hanover. The origin of the Church there differed from much of Presbyterianism in the South; it did not originate in a "Presbyterian community" made up of Scotch-Irish people who came to America from Scotland by way of Ireland. The people of Hanover, of English descent, experienced a spontaneous revival led by a layman, Samuel Morris, who gathered people in his home to read religious books. Soon these people heard of a New Side Presbyterian minister preaching in central and western Virginia. He must come their way! They sent messengers with an urgent invitation. So William Robinson in 1743 came for four "glorious days of the Son of Man."[2] After his departure other evangelists of the Presbytery of New Castle of the Synod of New York made brief visits, and were usually greatly inconvenienced by the restrictions placed on those not of the Church of England. These evangelists were but predecessors of the man who was a father of Presbyterianism in Virginia as well as elsewhere in the South.

SAMUEL DAVIES, FATHER OF HANOVER PRESBYTERY

Samuel Davies, a product of American Presbyterian revivalism, was the first moderator of Hanover Presbytery. The position was a testimony to the leadership he had given to the cause of Presbyterianism in Virginia. Born of Welsh parents in Delaware and trained in Pennsylvania, he was ordained in 1747 by New Castle Presbytery to visit congregations in Hanover County for six weeks. After this period he journeyed to Maryland and planned to accept a call in Delaware. But Virginia Presbyterians gave him no rest. They sent a petition, signed by one hundred and fifty heads of families in Hanover, urging Davies to become their pastor. Though broken in health, he decided to spend his remaining strength among the "pious and inquiring people" of Hanover, and "to expire under the fatigues of duty."[3]

When Samuel Davies first came to Virginia for six weeks in 1747, he traveled to Williamsburg to obtain the right to preach. Ministers who were not of the Church of England faced difficulty in securing a license. It appeared that great effort was made to limit the number of dissenting preachers (that is, those not of the State Church) and the number of preaching places such a minister might have. Davies stood before the Governor and his council. Almost a miracle! He was licensed! News reached Hanover before Davies arrived, not only that he was coming but that he was coming "qualified"!

When Davies returned to Virginia as pastor in 1748 he brought with him a young assistant, John Rodgers, who was to become the first moderator when a General Assembly of the Presbyterian Church was formed in later years. Davies and Rodgers appeared before the governor and the council. Rodgers was denied a license, and Davies was threatened with having his papers withdrawn. Such hindrances were not unusual. Some of the members in Hanover had been repeatedly fined for attending meetings of the Presbyterians. Hundreds of members who came into the Church had no minister or meeting house allowed them. These conditions led Davies to one of his greatest contributions, the struggle for religious toleration. On his heart was the "necessity of the dissenters."[4] He argued for them before the courts and used his pen to plead their case. When he visited England on behalf of the Presbyterian College of New Jersey, he laid the matter before the Attorney General and won concessions for his people. Religious liberty was not yet granted, but Davies' statement of the case for toleration, the service of Presbyterians in the French and Indian War, the aid of the Baptists, and the support of political leaders were factors that led to full religious freedom in 1786.

In spite of all difficulties Davies remained a true patriot. When General Braddock was defeated in 1755 and Virginia lay open to Indian attack, Davies called on the people of Hanover to stand firm in the "patriotism of true religion." "I am particularly solicitous that you, my brethren of the dissenters, should act with honor and spirit at this juncture, as it becomes loyal subjects, lovers of your country, and courageous Christians."[5] In a famous sermon, "The Curse of Cowardice," he presented the argument for self-defense and called for enlistment. "Our frontiers have been drenched with the blood of our fellow subjects, through the length of a thousand miles: and new wounds are still opening. . . . Now, perhaps, while I am speaking; now, while you are secure and unmolested, our fellow-subjects there may be feeling the calamities I am describing. . . . By the desertion of our remote settlements, the frontiers are approaching every day nearer and nearer to us; and if we cannot stand our ground now, when we have above a hundred miles of a thick-settled country between us and the enemy, much less shall we be able when our strength is weakened by so vast a loss of men, arms and riches, and we be exposed to their immediate incursions. . . . Let us then, in the name of the Lord of Hosts, the God of the Armies of Israel, let us collect our whole strength, and give one decisive blow; and we may humbly hope victory will be ours."[6]

Davies' greatest contribution was as a churchman. He was not a narrow denominationalist but labored and worked for the whole Church of Christ. "I am not fond, sir, of disseminating sedition and schism; I have no ambition to Presbyterianize the colony. But I may declare . . . that I have a sincere zeal, however languid and impotent, to propagate the catholic religion of Jesus in its life and power; though I feel but little anxiety about the denomination its genuine members assume."[7] He was one of the greatest preachers of his day, and to hundreds, and on occasions to more than a thousand, he tried to preach "as if I were to step from the pulpit to the supreme tribunal."[8] There are many testimonies to his visits in homes where he instructed and catechized, and to his interest in securing and distributing religious books. He was also one of the great and early American apostles to the slaves. About three hundred "poor neglected negroes" regularly attended his services. A hundred had been baptized and he recalled occasions when forty or more were gathered around the Lord's Table. On Saturday evening his home was crowded with them, and their singing was such as he could not forget. "Sometimes when I waked about two or three o'clock in the morning, a torrent of sacred harmony poured into my chamber, and carried my mind away to heaven."[9]

Though his parish was about ninety miles wide, Davies ministered to the whole of it and also made long missionary journeys to other places. These trips took him away so much that the elders asked Presbytery to refrain from assigning these duties. To meet the need and demand for preaching, Davies labored to bring in other ministers. He almost succeeded in winning the famous Jonathan Edwards for Virginia. Three of the six ministers who were formed into Hanover Presbytery had been secured by Davies and were working under his oversight. He was a great missionary statesman.

"It was in my heart to live and die with you," Davies said to his people in 1759 as he announced his acceptance of the presidency of the College of New Jersey. But the call, pressed three times, won from him the "conviction of duty."[10] He lived only two years at that post. A fitting epitaph is from one of the hymns he composed.

> Almighty grace, my soul inspire
> And touch my lips with heavenly fire.[11]

OLD SIDE AND NEW SIDE MISSIONARIES AMONG THE SCOTCH-IRISH

Hanover Presbytery was the result of the missionary labors of the New Side ministers of the Synod of New York, like Samuel Davies, who preached the "New Birth" and stressed revivalism. But there were other Presbyterians in Virginia. At the time Hanover was organized in 1755 with six ministers, there were three pastors in western Virginia who were not a part of this presbytery, because they belonged to the Old Side Synod of Philadelphia. This work in western Virginia was among the thousands of Scotch-Irish people who were filling up the great valley in that state. The Scotch-Irish had come a long way! In the north of Ireland there was a large body of Presbyterians who came from Scotland or were descendants of emigrants from Scotland. After 1715 these Scotch-Irish began to move in great numbers to America because of religious and economic conditions. It is estimated that two hundred thousand arrived between 1725 and 1768. Most of these settled in Pennsylvania. In about 1730 they began to move down into western Virginia. Attracted by advertisements of the beauty, fertility, and low cost of the land, welcomed as a bulwark against the Indians, and allowed a measure of freedom in their worship out on the frontier, they soon were the largest group in that area.

These settlers on the frontier received itinerating Presbyterian missionaries. Both Old Side and New Side Presbyterian ministers came. Sometimes neighboring congregations adhered to a different group, and at times there was division within a congregation. The Old Side Synod of Philadelphia placed three pastors among these Scotch-Irish settlers. The most noted was the Rev. John Craig. Born in Ireland, and educated in Edinburgh, he came to America in 1734. After being licensed by presbytery he was sent to Virginia, and he found there "the plot in Christ's vineyard, where I was to labor. . . . I thought God had given me a difficult plot to labor in, but I ever called upon Him in trouble, and He never failed to help."[12] In 1740 Craig became the first settled pastor in western Virginia, serving the Triple Forks of the Shenandoah Congregation, with two centers of worship—Augusta and Tinkling Spring. For thirty-four years he preached in the Valley. In the beginning he found his people "few and poor, and without order."[13] He left them "a numerous, wealthy congregation, able to support the gospel, and of credit and reputation in the church."[14]

These Scotch-Irish people who came into the Southern colonies were to constitute the major element for the growth of Presbyterianism in the South. Southern Presbyterianism is a happy blending of many strains of Presbyterians. Many nations aided its growth. "The courtly and cultivated Huguenots [from France], the stern and simple-hearted Highlander [from Scotland], the strong, the earnest, faithful Scotch-Irish, the conscientious Puritan [from England and Wales], and the frank, honest Teuton [from Germany, Holland, and Switzerland], contributed of the wealth of their character, and the glory of their history."[15] But the largest strain was that of Scotch-Irish people. They were "remarkable for the great simplicity of their manners, the plainness of their dress, and their frugal manner of living . . . they are strangers to luxury and refinement . . . brought up in habits of labor and industry, and scarce of money, they are for the most part clothed in homespun, nourished by the produce of their own farms, and happily appear to have neither taste nor inclination for high and expensive living. There is a quiet degree of equality among them. By far the greater part are in what might be called the middle station of life. None are very rich, few extremely poor. There are few slaves among them and these are treated with great kindness and humanity."[16]

Their lives centered in their churches. Worship was simple. The Church of Scotland was their model, although its forms were not slavishly followed. The use of Psalms was customary, but there was dispute about the version. Some preferred the Psalms in meter used in Scotland, although the trend was toward a modernization prepared by Watts and the use of hymns. The preaching of the Word was the heart of their worship. On the Sabbath there were two sermons, with a brief recess for lunch between the two.

The great days were the "sacramental occasions," the observance of the Lord's Supper. Usually held twice a year, the Communion season was a time when several congregations and ministers joined together. It was a social as well as religious occasion. On Friday the people began to gather, and there was a service of worship. On Saturday there was preaching, a short recess, and more preaching. The people assembled on Sunday at an earlier hour than usual, meeting sometimes in the nearby grove. If the worship were in the church building, ministers and elders were gathered in seats around the pulpit and reading desk. Long tables, extending to the right and left of the pulpit and down the aisle to the doors, were covered with white linen. First, there was the "Action Sermon" on the death of Christ and its fruits for the salvation of sinners. Then occurred the fencing of the table, a warning to the unprepared and impenitent to keep back from the Communion. A part of the congregation presented their tokens to the elders to show that they had been examined and admitted to the sacrament, and sat around the table as they were served the elements. Others followed until all were served, usually a different minister presiding at the table for each group. On Monday the pastor preached a sermon "calculated to cherish the impressions made on the minds of the people by the services of the preceding days."[17] There are several records of two thousand people being present for these sacramental occasions with about one in ten receiving Communion, a testimony to the proportion of the population who were not church members.

The nurture and care of the congregation was exercised by pastor and elders. Members were divided into "quarters" or "divisions," each under the oversight of an elder. Once a year the pastor and elders visited each family for an examination of life and knowledge. Often pastors arranged for a special meeting at the church to question their people, and some pastors submitted written questions in advance on which the members were to be prepared. The elders made up the session, which sometimes sat as a moral court to inquire into reports of unbecoming conduct.

The pastor was the shepherd of the flock. Frequently he was schoolteacher as well as preacher. When called by a congregation he was promised a salary based on subscriptions pledged by heads of families. A part of the salary was sometimes paid in wheat, corn, and other commodities. There is ample evidence of the small and uncertain pay of ministers and the poverty and distress of their widows and children. Many of the "pious ministers" struggled and earned their living by the sweat of their brows, while through the grace of God they preached the gospel.

The minister was a member of Presbytery. His "theological" training was usually supervised by an older minister. Requirements for licensure and ordination were exacting. The Rev. John Craig was assigned preliminary trial parts, judicial trial parts for licensure, then two years of supply work, followed by trial parts for ordination. The Rev. John Martin on March 18, 1756, delivered a discourse before Presbytery on Ephesians 2:1, and was examined on religious experience, reasons for desiring the ministry, Latin and Greek languages, and briefly on logic, ontology, ethics, natural philosophy, rhetoric, geography, and astronomy! Later, before a committee of Presbytery, he delivered a sermon on First Corinthians 1:22, 23 and a discussion of the question, *Num Revelatio supernaturalis sit necessaria* (Whether supernatural revelation is necessary). He prepared for another meeting of Presbytery a sermon on Galatians 2:2 and an exposition of Isaiah 61:1, 2, but delivered them before "some members in a private capacity." For the next meeting of Presbytery, August 25, he prepared a sermon on First John 5:16, and was further examined "in sundry extempore questions upon various branches of learning and divinity."[18] After he was licensed, there were other parts for ordination! Presbytery was quick to investigate evil reports about ministers, and it took action on unbecoming behavior, contention, failure to observe the law of the Church, preaching other men's sermons, and absenteeism from church courts.

REUNION OF OLD SIDE AND NEW SIDE: TREMENDOUS GROWTH

In 1758 the division among American Presbyterians was healed. New Side and Old Side were united in the one Synod of New York and Philadelphia. The division had been costly for the South, for it hindered missionary expansion among the Scotch-Irish and other people. With the reunion in 1758, the Old Side and New Side ministers in Virginia joined together in the Presbytery of Hanover. This prepared the way for missionary expansion. The growth of Presbyterianism in the South is reflected in the establishment of new presbyteries. Orange Presbytery, covering the Carolinas, was set off in 1770. South Carolina Presbytery was established in 1784. Abingdon Presbytery, covering Tennessee and Kentucky, and Lexington Presbytery in western Virginia were organized in 1785. In 1786 Transylvania Presbytery was set up for Kentucky.

Growth was the result of missionary enthusiasm and concern. The ministers were few in number, the shortage due in part to insistence of the Church on a highly select and well-trained ministry. Every effort was made to use the few ministers available in such a way as to meet the increasing demand and opportunity. Settled pastors were directed by Presbytery to devote some of their time to visiting communities which had no minister, and young ministers were licensed for a period of supply on the frontier. The great agent in the expansion was Hanover Presbytery. The beginning of Presbyterianism in the adjacent states was largely the result of the labors of its ministers, and the young leaders in those states for the most part were men licensed and ordained by this presbytery. But missionary expansion in the South was not a venture of Virginia Presbyterianism alone. The Synod of New York and Philadelphia sent out missionary teams, and the presbyteries of the middle colonies sent itinerants. Perhaps the greatest help was rendered by the Synod's school, the College of New Jersey. Until the establishment of Presbyterian colleges in the South, the college at Princeton provided the training for a large part of the ministry for the new areas.

Expansion was chiefly by means of missionary tours. Such a tour was made by the Rev. Hugh McAden in North Carolina. He was licensed by New Castle Presbytery in 1755 for missionary duty. His journal records his experiences, including his reactions on visits to about fifty settlements in North Carolina. While he preached to all groups, he was particularly drawn to the Scottish settlements in the eastern part of the state, and to the Scotch-Irish settlements in the western section. He was "alone in the wilderness," "sometimes a house in ten miles, and sometimes not that." On visiting a divided congregation he wrote, "O may the good Lord, who can bring order out of confusion . . . visit this people." The Gaelic-speaking Scottish Presbyterians around Fayetteville impressed him: "Some of them scarcely knew one word that I said,—the poorest singers I ever heard in all my life." He was "resolved not to be so anxious about getting along in my journey, but take some more time to labor among the people." If his horse turned up sick or lame he stayed several days. All the time he was preaching, and praying, "May the Lord . . . grant his blessing upon my poor attempts, and make me in some way instrumental in turning some of these precious souls from darkness unto light."[19] After his missionary tour McAden returned to the state to serve Presbyterians near Wilmington and later in Caswell County near the Virginia line. By that time other ministers had arrived, including the famous Alexander Craighead whose efforts aided Presbyterian growth around Charlotte.

Hugh McAden also visited South Carolina. The growth of Presbyterianism in that state was chiefly among the Scotch-Irish, who moved down from the North or who arrived from Ireland by way of Charleston. It was largely the result of the missionary activities of the presbyteries which were a part of the Synod of New York and Philadelphia. These missionaries came in contact with a presbytery of the Church of Scotland formed around Charleston before 1722. This Presbytery of Charleston was much older than Hanover, but, for reasons already stated, of far less significance in Southern Presbyterianism. After several decades of existence apart from the mainstream of American Presbyterianism, it became a part of that mainstream after the formation of the General Assembly. Its strength was among the Scottish people who had settled near Charleston. The founder of that presbytery was Archibald Stobo. A minister of the Church of Scotland, he was returning from Panama when shipwreck landed him on the South Carolina coast. In Charleston and the surrounding areas he labored, such a decided Presbyterian that he did not get along well with Congregationalists, with whom the Presbyterians worshiped at that time. He was famous for his "protracted services." On one occasion a Huguenot (a Presbyterian from France) listened to Stobo's sermon until dinnertime, left the church, and returned after his meal to hear the rest of the sermon! But Stobo was a worker, and the permanency of Presbyterianism around

Charleston owed much to his labors. Some of the ministers who were licensed by Hanover or other presbyteries of the Synod of New York and Philadelphia joined the Presbytery of Charleston for work in South Carolina.

Presbyterians moved into Georgia. In Savannah a congregation of the Church of Scotland was formed in 1755 and still exists as the Independent Presbyterian Church. Congregationalists from New England arrived and some became Presbyterians. Scotch-Irish moved into the state from the Carolinas. Soon missionaries answered their appeal. But little was accomplished until after the War of Independence.

In Tennessee the Rev. Charles Cummings and the Rev. Joseph Rhea were the first to preach the gospel. Cummings journeyed there from his parish in western Virginia. On Sunday mornings he would dress himself, put on his bullet pouch, mount his horse, and with rifle in hand ride off to one of his churches.[20] The Rev. Samuel Doak, "apostle of learning and religion in the west," and probably the first settled pastor in Tennessee, labored in establishing churches and schools and two colleges. On commencement days, in later years, "he wore his antique wig, his shorts, and his old-fashioned shoes: the muscles of his stern brow were relaxed, and he gave himself up to an unusual urbanity and kindliness of manner."[21] In Kentucky the leader was David Rice who moved to that "dark and bloody ground" in 1783 and soon earned the title of "Father Rice." He established churches at Danville and other places, led in education, and was vigorous in his opposition to slavery. About the same time the Rev. John McCue was preaching in what is now West Virginia. These pioneer missionaries labored under great hardships; their reward was to see the Church established in new areas.

SOUTHERN PRESBYTERIANS IN THE NATION'S WAR FOR INDEPENDENCE

During these years of missionary expansion the colonies became involved in the War of Independence. This war has been called a "Presbyterian Rebellion." Not all Presbyterians favored independence before the conflict began. Once the war started, however, it received their strong support. There was no war-mongering in the meetings of the church courts; on the other hand, there was no hesitancy about making declarations on the events of the time. The Synod of New York and Philadelphia addressed a pastoral letter in 1766. "You will not forget to honor your king, and pay a due submission to his august parliament . . . a spirit of liberty is highly laudable when under proper regulations, but we hope you will carefully distinguish between liberty and licentiousness!"[22] When war had begun the Synod recommended attachment and respect "to our Sovereign King," maintenance of union among the colonies, strictness of life and government in the churches, "a regard to order and the public peace," "a spirit of humanity and mercy," and their continuing "habitually in the exercise of prayer."

In the South, sentiment for independence was strong. The Presbyterians around Charlotte in North Carolina drew up in 1775 their Mecklenburg Resolutions, looking toward independence. Hanover Presbytery was the first Church body to approve "sentiments" of the Declaration of Independence. On the basis of the Virginia Declaration of Rights it asked for full religious liberty in Virginia. "We ask no ecclesiastical establishments for ourselves; neither can we approve of them when granted to others."[23] Presbyterians went forth as generals and privates. Ministers accompanied the troops. The Rev. James Hall of North Carolina, for example, served as captain and chaplain. He rode through the Carolinas "with his three-cornered hat and long sword, the captain at the head of a company, and chaplain of the regiment."[24] The war brought much suffering. Presbyterians in Virginia and North Carolina, known for their strong sentiments for independence, were given "special" treatment. The evidence was in "our burnt and wasted churches, and our plundered dwellings." They had inherited from Presbyterian ancestors the doctrine of the right to resist, but they sought to carry out their part in the civil strife as Christians.

EARLY PRESBYTERIAN SCHOOLS

The record of the Presbyterians in the war is testimony to their participation in the life of the nation. The Presbyterian influence in the social and political life was exercised through those nurtured in Presbyterian churches and trained in Presbyterian schools. Local schools, classical academies, and finally colleges were established by Presbyterians. Many pastors circulated libraries and combined schoolteaching with preaching. David Caldwell established a famous classical school in North Carolina; in that same state Samuel Eusebius McCorkle conducted his "Zion-Parnassus," and James Hall had "Clio's Nursery." North Carolina Presbyterians founded Queens Museum, later called Liberty Hall. Cambridge Academy and Mt. Zion College in South Carolina were largely Presbyterian schools. In Virginia, Augusta Academy was taken over by Hanover Presbytery and became Liberty Hall, then Washington College, now Washington and Lee University. The Presbytery also founded Hampden-Sydney College. The ambitious program of these schools is indicated by an early announcement of Hampden-Sydney Academy. There "shall be taught the Greek and Latin languages to their greatest extent; and all the sciences which are usually studied, at any College, or Academy, on the Continent. He [the director] proposes to teach Geography in greater perfection than . . . is done in the major parts of our Institutions of learning; and so as to render it an excellent handmaid to the extensive and useful study of History; which with the science of Chronology shall be attended to. Mathematical learning he has made himself master of; and designs to teach those who choose, Arithmetic and Algebra; and Geometry applied particularly to surveying. This will prepare the way for the study of Natural Philosophy in all its branches; after which he will instruct them in the important studies of Eloquence, Criticism, and the Science of Morals."[25]

THE FORMATION OF THE GENERAL ASSEMBLY

After the war Presbyterianism in the nation and in the South progressed until a single synod was no longer adequate. This was a period of constitution-making and formation of national organizations in Churches and the nation. Proposals for a General Assembly met with acceptance by Southern presbyteries. The first General Assembly of the Presbyterian Church in the United States of America was formed in 1788. It consisted of four synods: the Synod of New York and New Jersey, the Synod of Philadelphia, the Synod of Virginia, and the Synod of the Carolinas. The Synod of Virginia had thirty ministers in four presbyteries: Hanover, Redstone (in western Pennsylvania), Lexington, and Transylvania. The Synod of the Carolinas had twenty-five ministers in the Presbyteries of Orange, Abingdon, and South Carolina. These Southern synods and presbyteries were a part of the Presbyterian Church in America and a part of the family of Presbyterian Churches of the world.

Growing Pains

T
HE GENERAL ASSEMBLY of the Presbyterian Church in America held its first meeting in 1789. In that same year George Washington began his service as president of the United States. The Church was ready for life in the new nation. It had adopted a discipline and government "accommodated to the state of the Presbyterian Church in America." A Catechism and Confession of Faith had been approved, and a Directory of Worship "more suitable to our circumstances and tastes than any we yet have."[1]

The Presbyterian Church compared well with other religious groups. Though statistics were hard to keep, could any other Church claim a larger membership or greater influence? Probably only one, the Congregational Church, but how soon a change was to take place! As early as 1800 the Presbyterians were outstripped in numbers by two other groups, and Presbyterian impact on the life of the nation diminished. This loss was but the harvest of conditions of long standing. The shortage of ministers had been acute. Requirement of college and "seminary" education made for highly trained ministers, but how few they were! Despite pleas from areas destitute of churches, the Church adhered to this policy as the wisest course. These educated preachers were well equipped for schoolteaching; thus much ministerial time was used up and preachers were localized. Not that the Presbyterian ministers did not itinerate, but they were no match for the Methodists—"While the good Presbyterian parson was writing his discourses . . . the Methodist itinerant had traveled forty miles with his horse and saddle bags . . ."[2] The Presbyterian ministers preached to all hearers but usually settled where a sufficient number of Scotch-Irish folk issued a call. The call promised a salary, and this "salaried" Presbyterian parson was made the object of ridicule by the Baptist farmer-preacher and the Methodist circuit rider. Also contributing to the Presbyterian decline was the loss of the great New Side evangelistic fervor preceding and during the war.

But the decline was not evident in 1789. The Presbyterians faced confidently the challenge of the new day. There was a multitude of unreached people, less than one person in ten being a church member. Of this multitude the war had taken its moral toll; concerns of this life occupied their attention, and indifference to Christianity was widespread. Irreligion was on the increase. Deism, accepting the moral principles of Christianity but despising "revealed religion," was popular. Amidst such conditions, when "silence would be criminal," the General Assembly spoke: "We desire to direct your awakened attention toward that bursting storm which threatens to sweep before it the religious principles, institutions, and morals of our people. We are filled with deep concern and awful dread . . ."[3] Against these forces the Presbyterian Church used its strength.

FOLLOWING PIONEERS TO THE FRONTIER

Many people were moving to vast new areas. Down the Ohio, over the mountains, through the Cumberland Gap, the settlers poured. Ohio, Kentucky, and Tennessee were filling up with inhabitants. Pioneers moved to the edge of the frontier. Farmers with only bare necessities arrived to build one-room log cabins. They lived in isolation, often seized with fear as they listened during long hours for the approach of Indians. But the abundance of land brought people by the thousands. Soon there were little settlements with stores and taverns, and by 1821 nine new states had been added to the Union.

Frontiers new and old received the attention of the Presbyterians. The first Assembly had requested each synod to recommend "two members, well-qualified to be employed in Missions on our frontiers." Presbyteries were "strictly enjoined" to take "collections" for this work. In 1794 the Assembly sent a circular letter to "inhabitants visited by the missionaries," voicing its concern over "the state of our frontier and other settlements in the Union, which are destitute of the regular administration of the worship and ordinances of God." It was "desirous to do all in our power to extend the blessings of the gospel amongst you . . . As our aim has not been to proselyte from other communities to our denomination, we have charged our missionaries to avoid all doubtful disputations, to abstain from unfriendly censures or reflections on other religious persuasions . . ."[4] Later the Assembly enjoined presbyteries to collect information about Indian tribes, frontier settlements, interior districts destitute of the means of grace, the "colored race," and proper persons to be missionaries in any of these areas. In 1801 the Presbyterians joined with the Congregationalists in a "Plan of Union" for co-operation, not competition, in serving the frontier, and in 1802 organized the "Standing Committee of Missions."

This concern for the unreached was shared by the synods and presbyteries in the South. Both the Synod of Virginia and the Synod of the Carolinas assumed responsibility for missions within their bounds and each formed a Commission of Synod to conduct the enterprise. Presbyteries licensed young men, put them under the care and direction of the Commission of Synod, and raised contributions for their labors. The Commission in Virginia sent out three missionaries in 1791. In that same year the Synod of the Carolinas sent out four missionaries, directed them "not to tarry longer than three weeks at the same time in the bounds of twenty miles, except peculiar circumstances may appear to make it necessary."[5] By 1802 there was a report to the Assembly, "the prospects of success—are flattering, as well among the Indians as among the frontier whites."[6]

The place on the frontier which witnessed the most rapid growth lay within the bounds of the Synod of Virginia. A part of that synod was set off in 1802 as the Synod of Pittsburgh. But there was still much territory left—southern Ohio and all of Kentucky! Virginia sent settlers and ministers into Kentucky. "Father Rice" had gone over in 1783 and led in the formation of Transylvania Presbytery in 1786. Presbyterianism made rapid progress. The cause—revival!

BLESSINGS AND TRIALS OF REVIVAL

The Kentucky revival came from Virginia. It started in a church school, Hampden-Sydney College, which shared in the irreligion that spread after the War of Independence. "Religion and religious persons" were treated with ridicule and contempt. The few students who were "serious and thoughtful" kept religious interests secret "for fear of persecution and ridicule." All of this was a heavy burden on the heart of the president, Dr. John Blair Smith. With elders of two nearby churches he began to pray. The prayers were answered in the conversion of one student, Carey Allen. Soon there were four, and then student prayer meetings filled the college hall. A revival was under way! It spread to nearby counties. Ministers and congregations came a distance of a hundred miles to see the miracle. The revival spread to the neighboring Washington College, and at both schools there was an outpouring of young life for the ministry.

Among those who witnessed the revival was the Rev. James McGready. He carried the emphasis to his new work in North Carolina. Here extraordinary events took place, but his preaching was "running people distracted." The opposition led him to move to Kentucky, where the revival took root. God was "shaking the valley of dry bones on the frontiers. The few scattering drops before a mighty rain" were only the beginning; soon there was an "overwhelming flood of salvation."[7]

To aid in the revival in Kentucky the Presbyterians developed the "camp meeting." At first the camp meeting did not appear too different from the sacramental occasions which lasted several days. With so much evidence of God's favor about, people came from long distances. No building could hold such numbers. Why not an outdoor setting where thousands could hear, could camp nearby and stay for days? So the camp meeting began. An encampment was formed. Near the center was a large vacant area with rude platforms or pulpits. One camp meeting attracted twenty-five thousand people and twenty-five preachers who exhorted day and night! There were strange sights and sounds: "the glare of the blazing camp-fires falling on a dense assemblage of heads . . . bowed in adoration, and reflected back from long ranges of tents upon every side; hundreds of candles and lamps suspended amid the trees . . . the solemn chanting of hymns swelling and falling on the night wind; the impassioned exhortations; the earnest prayers, the sobs, shrieks, or shouts . . ."[8]

Under such prolonged excitement there were unbelievable happenings. People by the hundreds, of all denominations, "fell" and remained stiff and in a stupor. Some took the "jerks" and could not control their limbs or head. Involuntary barking and dancing seized others. No wonder some preachers felt led to preach on "Bodily exercise profiteth little," or "Let all things be done decently and in order"!

Presbyterians experienced rapid growth. The Kentucky revival spread—to Tennessee, Virginia, and the Carolinas. It became a part of the general revivalism that was sweeping the nation—New England, the colleges of the East, western New York. The first third of the century witnessed one revival after another.

In spite of growth Presbyterians were not entirely happy. Not everything about revivals was good. People in Kentucky knew this. At first there was appreciation for revivals, with a disposition to pardon their irregularities. But very soon the Kentucky Presbyterians were divided, revivalists and anti-revivalists. For some the revival "resembled the whirlwind, the earthquake, the impetuous torrent, whose track was marked by violence and desolation." Before it was over several groups left the Presbyterian Church.

The great loss was that of the Cumberland Presbyterians in Kentucky and Tennessee. The rupture was due to differences over the method, agents, and theology of revival. There had been a harvest of new members. To provide preaching for the many new congregations, the revivalists favored licensing and ordaining men without the normal educational qualifications.

Especially in Cumberland Presbytery, where the revivalists were in control, was the requirement for "classical learning" relaxed; and there were licensed men of good character who had proved their acceptability to the churches. Anti-revivalists were accused of "making men gentlemen before [they] made them ministers."[9] These "uneducated" ministers exhorted "wherever God in his providence called them," and thus appeared as "Methodist circuit riders," without sufficient respect for the bounds of established congregations. The licensing of "illiterate exhorters," after examination on "experimental religion" and motive for entering the ministry and demonstration of ability to deliver a discourse, led to the condemnation of Cumberland Presbytery by Synod and caused a conflict over the rights and powers in the examination of ministers—whether under Presbyterian law the examination belonged to synod or presbytery. This conflict was further complicated by the issue of doctrine. Cumberland Presbytery received candidates who accepted the Confession of Faith only to the extent that "they believed it to agree with the word of God." They objected to sections on infant damnation, double predestination, limited atonement, and perseverance of the saints, laid stress on free will, and approached the Methodist doctrine of grace. The Presbytery was condemned by the Synod of Kentucky, and the General Assembly, swayed by the oratory of John Lyle and the Presbytery's failure to follow orderly procedures in presenting its case, gave unanimous endorsement to the action! As a result there was formed the Cumberland Presbyterian Church. It had its beginning in 1810 and by 1829 had a General Assembly.

Many thought that this was a tragic loss for the Presbyterian Church in America. Cumberland Presbyterians increased far more rapidly than the regular Presbyterians in Kentucky and Tennessee. Their zeal was sorely missed. They did not abandon educational qualifications for the ministry, nor did they become arch-heretics. If their doctrinal views were a denial of some of the tenets of the Church, had not these same doctrines caused many others difficulty? Did not their irregularities in church order stem from burning zeal? Would they not have been corrected if met with patience and discretion? Would not a less stiff-backed attitude and more love have saved for the Presbyterian Church in America the zeal of thousands of the poor and unedu-cated people? So thought many at that time.

MISSIONARY EXPANSION AT HOME AND ABROAD

In spite of troubles the era of revivalism continued. With it went an expanding missionary enterprise and the development of the Church's missionary agencies. The Standing Committee of Missions of 1802 became the Board of Missions of 1816. The Western Missionary Society of the Synod of Pittsburgh, formed in 1802, became the Western Foreign Missionary Society in 1831 and the Presbyterian Board of Foreign Missions in 1837. The Presbyterian Church did not conduct its work only through denominational agencies. The first thirty years of the nineteenth century were an era of co-operative effort. Presbyterians joined with the Congregationalists in the Plan of Union in 1801 to meet the needs of the frontier. With the Dutch Reformed Church and Associate Reformed Church they formed the United For-eign Missionary Society in 1817, and in 1826 this became a part of a larger co-operative work, the American Board of Commis-sioners for Foreign Missions. They supported the United Domes-tic Missionary Society and its sequel, the American Home Mis-sionary Society, and shared in the American Sunday School Union and the American Tract Society.

Participation in interdenominational work was based in part on the theory that missionary work was optional and that those interested might form societies for its promotion. But is not mis-sions the very business of the Church? So thought the Synod of Pittsburgh. This view won increasing acceptance until in 1831 Dr. John Holt Rice of Virginia sent an overture to the General Assembly: "Be it resolved . . . that the Presbyterian Church in the United States is a missionary society; the object of which is to aid in the conversion of the world; and that every member of the church is a member for life of said society, and bound, in maintenance of his Christian character, to do all in his power for the accomplishment of this object."[10] This view was to triumph in the Presbyterian Church.

Presbyterian missionary expansion in the South was the result of labors of Assembly agencies and interdenominational societies, together with synod and presbytery agencies and local missionary societies. The "importunate cries . . . for missionaries, the cry of souls ready to perish" brought tremendous response. Meetings of presbytery, synod, and Assembly were filled with missionary sermons, missionary reports, and missionary "collections."

The agent was the missionary. There are numerous records of trials, hardships, exceedingly low pay, dedication, zeal, and reactions of missionaries to these experiences. William Hill of Virginia recorded in his journal in 1790: "Rode constantly all day. Tarried at night at a tavern . . . Fatigued with my day's work— in a cold winter's night—in a land of strangers."[11] The Rev. James Hall of North Carolina visited Mississippi in 1800. "Only one Episcopalian, one Methodist, and two Baptist clergymen, besides a few exhorters . . . are in the Territory!"[12] He and his two companions were praised for their preaching, "omitting points barely speculative, you have insisted on points radical and essential."[13] A missionary in Kentucky confided in his journal, "preached to a considerable number of people. I delivered a very lengthy discourse, yet love, and unremitted attention was given."[14] The Rev. Jeremiah Chamberlain, one of the fathers of Presbyterianism in Mississippi, received his instructions from the Assembly's Board of Missions: "Mr. Jeremiah Chamberlain, six months through the Southwestern Counties of Pennsylvania to the Ohio River, and down that river to St. Louis, where he will join Mr. Larned, and then visit the destitute towns on the Mississippi between Natchez and New Orleans, and, if practicable, visit the settlements on the Mobile"![15] The Mr. Larned mentioned was the Rev. Sylvester Larned who founded Presbyterianism in New Orleans. No sooner had he arrived than he began to preach. Here are "dear children of God,—how many, I have . . . no means of ascertaining."[16] Eighteen months after his arrival he was dead of fever. Hugh Wilson, commissioned as a missionary to Texas in 1837, was told, "It is incumbent on you to cultivate a spirit of kindness toward all the family of Christ of every name, and carefully avoid contention and both public and private debate of a sectarian nature." [17]

One of the great missionaries was Daniel Baker, whose labors touched so much of the South. He was an outstanding revival preacher and a successful settled pastor. During his pastorate in Savannah his heart began "hankering after a missionary life." "But to be cut down from two thousand dollars to six hundred dollars was a serious affair . . . Was not the hand of God in this? It seemed to speak in tones from heaven, loud and distinct, 'Go forth as a missionary and preach the Gospel.' Accordingly . . . I resigned my charge." [18]

Presbyterianism in the South increased through these missionary labors—and those of many others. There were John Newton and Daniel Thatcher in Georgia, William McWhir in Florida, John McElhaney in (present-day) West Virginia, James L. Sloss in Alabama, Salmon Giddings and Timothy Flint in Missouri, James Wilson Moore in Arkansas, W. Y. Allen and John McCullough in Texas, Samuel A. Worcester in Oklahoma. Some were sent out by Presbyterian agencies in the North, some by those in the South. Some were commissioned by interdenominational agencies. They were men of broad and catholic spirit, with concern for "all the family of Christ." By 1838 they had reached all of the Southern states.

While the Presbyterian Church expanded to far frontiers, there were groups within the bounds of the Presbyterian Church who were objects of missionary concern. The "gospeling of the Indian" was not forgotten. Rev. Gideon Blackburn was commissioned by the Assembly's Standing Committee on Missions as its first missionary to the Indians for work in eastern Tennessee. "The Standing Committee on Missions acting under the authority, and by the order of, the General Assembly of the Presbyterian Church in the United States of America . . . have appointed you, the Revd. Gideon Blackburn their missionary to the Cherokee nation of Indians, for the purpose of carrying the gospel, and the arts of civilized life to them."[19] Cyrus Kingsbury also labored among the Cherokees in eastern Tennessee and western North Carolina, moved to work among the Choctaws of Mississippi, and later followed the Indians over the "trail of tears" to their new homes west of the Mississippi River. The Synod of South Carolina and Georgia established a mission among the Chickasaws in northern Mississippi. Their missionary, Thomas C. Stuart, experienced firsthand what it is "to form a settlement in the midst of a heathen people, far removed from civilized and Christian society . . . I was alone, I had no associate with whom to counsel, or who could sympathize with me in my trials."[20] Tombigbee Presbytery of the Synod of South Carolina and Georgia was formed in 1828 from workers among the Choctaws and Chickasaws. These workers established churches and schools. In addition to concern for the spiritual welfare of the Indians, they manifested interest in their physical well-being, expressing opposition to the removal of the Indians from territory they had long occupied.

The evangelization of Negroes was more a part of the work of settled pastors than of special missionaries. Neither group was very successful. Out of a quarter of a million Negro church members in the South only about seven thousand were Presbyterian in 1840. But there is evidence of the Church's concern for the Negroes' spiritual and physical welfare. The Assembly in 1794 urged that slaves not over fifteen years of age be taught to read the Word of God and be given such training as would prepare them to enjoy the benefits of freedom. In some states the Presbyterians sought to teach slaves to read in spite of state laws forbidding it. At times the Assembly commended presbyteries which had given special emphasis to evangelizing the Negroes; some presbyteries record their sorrow for their neglect of this duty. The Assembly in 1806 appointed Dr. John Holt Rice "a missionary for three months to the blacks of Charlotte county, Virginia, and parts adjacent."[21] A Negro, John Chavis, was a missionary under the direction of the General Assembly, and he settled in Lexington, Virginia, to labor "among people of his own color."

There were other Negro preachers, some of whom went to Africa as missionaries. In 1825 the Assembly declared that there was no more honored name than "apostle to our slaves." The great Presbyterian apostle to the slaves was a Southerner, Charles Colcock Jones. He gave up the pastorate of the First Presbyterian Church of Savannah, Georgia, to labor among and for the Negroes, and he became the agent of the Presbyterian Board of Domestic Missions for Colored Work in the South and Southwest. His *Catechism for the Oral Instruction of Colored Persons* was widely used. James Smylie of Mississippi also did successful work and prepared a catechism.

Thus the missionary labors progressed. After 1824 there was a decided shift in strategy from emphasis on itineration and establishing congregations to concentration on settling pastors and aiding congregations until they came to self-support. There were fewer missionary tours—and less growth. Sunday schools were promoted, with the aid of the Assembly's Board of Education formed in 1819. The churches exercised a strong moral influence, and the records of church sessions reveal the frequency and frankness with which problems of misbehavior were handled.

"Foreign" missionary concern was expressed chiefly in behalf of the Indians. Though it was not until 1831 that the Western Foreign Missionary Society was formed, which in 1837 became the Presbyterian Board of Foreign Missions, Presbyterians in the South went out under the interdenominational American Board of Commissioners for Foreign Missions, and continued to do so during this period as well as going out under the Western Foreign Missionary Society. Most of the Presbyterian missionaries in the South before 1838 went out under the American Board. Among the Presbyterians of the South who offered themselves, George W. Boggs sailed for India, James L. Merrick to Persia, John B. Adger and T. P. Johnson to Armenia, J. R. Lanneau to Syria, and S. R. Brown to China. John Brooks Pinney, John Leighton Wilson, Alexander Erwin Wilson, and Daniel Lindley sailed to Africa. The wife of Dr. Alexander Erwin Wilson, Jane Smithey Wilson, was the first white woman to be buried in the Transvaal. Samuel

R. Houston and George W. Leyburn went to Greece. The cause
of foreign missions was greatly promoted by a Society of Missionary Inquiry formed at Columbia Seminary and a similar organization at Union Seminary. The Southern Board of Foreign
Missions formed by the Synod of South Carolina in 1833 also
did notable work. Inspiration came through Dr. Thomas Smyth
of Charleston. His poor health kept him from the foreign field,
but the Second Presbyterian Church of Charleston, where he
organized a Juvenile Missionary Society, and the Synod of South
Carolina felt his concern and furnished personnel and funds for
the foreign field.

ESTABLISHMENT OF SOUTHERN SEMINARIES

The missionary outreach made more acute the shortage of
ministers. What was the Church to do? One step the Church
could take was to establish a seminary, and thus the Assembly's
Seminary at Princeton, New Jersey, opened its doors in 1812.
But Princeton was so far away. A seminary was needed in the
South. Even before the founding of Princeton, the Presbyterians
of Virginia had taken action. Theological training was given in
Liberty Hall Academy under the leadership of William Graham,
and by John McMillan in western Pennsylvania, then a part of
the Synod of Virginia. Later, in 1806, funds were raised for a
theological library and for a professorship of theology at Hampden-Sydney. But little that was permanent was accomplished until
Hanover Presbytery called John Holt Rice to the task. He believed that "the state of things in the South" was such that "a
theological seminary in the South is necessary . . . if there is not
one established before long the consequences will be very deplor-
able. The majority of students in the South will not go North."[22]
There was also fear of "training men for the South in the North
country" and of "the unfitness of most Northern men for our
purposes." Dr. Rice was the real founder of the seminary in
Virginia which in 1824 opened its doors as a separate institution
from Hampden-Sydney College and, with the assumption of con-

trol by the Synods of Virginia and North Carolina, was named "The Union Seminary." His ideal was "men all on fire, and at the same time . . . acquainted with the state of the world." He wanted to take young men "out of their dark corners and bring them into the Church through the seminary."[23] "Allow me, however," he wrote, "to say that in this Southern region, we do not want any body who thinks he has made new discoveries in religion . . . in a word, the people here know nothing of the *Isms* which have plagued you all to the North; and we do not wish them to know. But a man, who will just preach the Bible honestly and faithfully . . ."![24]

Soon another seminary was begun in the South. The Presbyterians of South Carolina and Georgia contributed generously to the support of the Assembly's Seminary at Princeton. But the distance of Princeton and the difference of habits and feelings appeared to justify and require a seminary for the "Southern Church." In 1817 the Presbytery of Hopewell proposed a seminary for the southeastern region, and the Presbytery of South Carolina even proposed a name, "The Classical, Scientific and Theological Seminary of the South"! The Synod of South Carolina and Georgia took over the project, and, "aware of the superior claims of the present age to an enlightened ministry,"[25] established "The Theological Seminary of the Synod of South Carolina and Georgia." Opening in 1828 at Lexington, Georgia, the seminary had one professor, five students, and no buildings! In 1830 it was moved to Columbia, South Carolina. In its early years it was aided by New England Puritans with faculty, students, and funds. One of the great contributions of New England was in the person of Dr. George Howe, who became Professor of Biblical Literature in 1831. When called in 1836 to the Professorship of Sacred Literature at Union Seminary in New York, he wrote, "It appears still my duty to cast my lot and earthly destiny with the people of the South . . . When I accepted the Professorship I hold, it was with the hope that I might be the means of building up the wastes, and extending the borders of our Southern Zion. This motive still holds me here. Though our institution must be a small one through the present generation, and yours will be large, it is important, it is necessary . . . that this Seminary should live. If I remain, though the field of my effort must be small, and I must live on in obscurity, we may yet transmit to the men of the next generation an institution which will bless them and the world."[26]

PROGRESS IN EDUCATION AND JOURNALISM

The interest in education was not confined to seminaries. Tusculum College in eastern Tennessee developed from one of the institutions founded by Samuel Doak. Southern and Western Theological Seminary, established in Tennessee in 1819, became Maryville College. Presbyterians of Kentucky established Transylvania Seminary, and when they lost control of that institution founded Centre College in 1819. Davidson College, established in 1837 by the Presbytery of Concord in North Carolina and the Presbytery of Bethel in South Carolina, was opened as a manual labor school. The Presbyterians of Georgia laid the foundation of Oglethorpe University, while Oakland College, now Chamberlain Hunt Academy, was built in Mississippi. A major purpose of these colleges was the "education of pious youth for the gospel ministry." Often great aid was given for this purpose by local educational societies formed by women in the churches. In addition to church schools Presbyterians were leaders in founding the University of North Carolina, the University of Georgia, and the University of Tennessee. An educated ministry and educational institutions continued to give Presbyterians a far greater influence in shaping the cultural life of the time than their numbers would indicate.

Along with interest in education there were efforts in religious journalism. Church papers carried news of the Christian world and denominational items, as well as articles on general topics. *The Virginia Religious Magazine* was begun in 1804 by a group of Presbyterian ministers "with the full support of Synod." The magazine was "the first of the kind, we believe, that has ever been published in this State, or in any of the States south of the Potomac."[27] John Holt Rice edited *The Christian Monitor* for two years and followed it with *The Virginia Evangelical and Literary Magazine.* Later in Richmond, Amasa Converse edited the *Southern Religious Telegraph.* In South Carolina, *The Southern Evangelical Intelligencer* was published by two Presbyterian ministers and was succeeded by *The Charleston Observer,* edited by the great Rev. Benjamin Gildersleve, who had been responsible for *The Missionary,* published in Georgia from 1819-1825. In Kentucky there was *The Western Luminary,* a journal with interdenominational character edited by a Presbyterian, Thomas Skillman, who also issued *The Presbyterian Advocate* for one year. Also in Kentucky were *The Temperance Herald of the Mississippi Valley* and *The Protestant and Herald.* In Tennessee *The Calvinistic Magazine* was commended for support. In addition *The Assembly's Missionary Magazine* was read, along with *The Home Missionary,* published by the interdenominational American Home Mission Society. Several Presbyterian papers in the South arose as a result of the tensions in the Church in the 1830's.

DIFFERENCES AND DIVISION: OLD SCHOOL AND NEW SCHOOL

The first third of the century witnessed rapid growth. Differences, sometimes resulting in loss of members, arose over revivals, Psalmody, slavery, and doctrine. At times the churches in the South, far from the centers of greater Presbyterian strength, felt neglected. But the South had contributed twelve Moderators of the General Assembly during the period. A spirit of good will and confidence filled the Church.

About 1830 a sharp change took place. Church leaders began to dispute, "some for *old* orthodoxy, some for *new* metaphysics." Everything appeared "cold and dead, except the spirit of controversy."[28] The Presbyterian Church became sharply and almost evenly divided into two camps, the "Old School" and the "New School." To some extent the division was related to national origins, as the Old School was largely made up of those with Scotch-Irish background, while the New School was strong in areas where the Presbyterians had New England or English background. There were several main issues: Was not Presbyterian government breaking down through the operation of the Plan of Union with the Congregationalists? Was not "heresy" coming into the Presbyterian Church through this same source and had it not infected a large portion of the New School group? Should not the Presbyterian Church conduct its work through denominational boards which it controlled rather than through interdenominational societies favored by the New School? All of these charges were made by the Old School. Another factor in the division was the attitude toward slavery. The increasing antislavery agitation was found chiefly in the New School areas. This fact helps to explain why more than three fourths of the Southern churches adhered to the Old School. Some in the South at this time wanted to get all Southerners, New School and Old School, together in a Southern Presbyterian Church.

In 1837 the Old School controlled the Assembly. The Plan of Union was abrogated as being unconstitutional (it had been in force since 1801). On the principle that "an unconstitutional act involves the unconstitutionality of all that is done under it," the Old School party, amid hissing from the galleries, cut off four synods, five hundred and thirty-three churches, and more than one hundred thousand members. The result was two Presbyterian denominations, almost the same size, with the same title, and each claiming to be the true continuation of the Presbyterian Church.

Presbyterian leaders in the South figured largely in the division. The 1837 pre-Assembly Convention of the Old School party was presided over by Dr. George Baxter. He and Dr. William S. Plumer, both of Virginia, took leading parts in the work of separating the Church into two bodies. Dr. Plumer was the first moderator of the Old School Church in 1838. Dr. Robert J. Breckinridge of Kentucky was the equal of any in activity against the New School. More than three fourths of the Southern churches adhered to the Old School Assembly. Some Southern presbyteries which continued with the Old School condemned the methods by which the division was effected. The Southern churches which joined the New School Assembly were located chiefly in Virginia, Kentucky, Tennessee, Mississippi, and Missouri.

The division was costly to the Presbyterian Church. Daniel Baker wrote: "Their wranglings grieved me much. I was wont to say, 'I have no horns; I know not how to fight; I am one of the working ants.' "[29] But division left no room for a "fence-man," and soon all took sides. The Presbyterians needed more men like John Holt Rice, who had believed "the Church is not to be purified by controversies but by holy love."[30] Many Old School leaders showed a rigid, stiff-backed attitude and a zeal for heresy-hunting, admitting no interpretation of the Standards other than their own. Their methods in cutting off four synods were unwise, if not worse. Many of the New School leaders were not only very liberal in theology for their day and at times appeared indifferent to the principles of Presbyterian government, but "taking counsel with extremists to the alienation of moderate men,"[31] refused to listen to the great "middle ground" of the Presbyterian Church and were determined to push their own program. The result of a lack of "holy love" was tragic.

CHAPTER III

"Our Southern Zion"

D IVISION OF THE PRESBYTERIAN CHURCH into Old School and New School was completed in 1838 with the organization of two Assemblies. The controversy and division weakened the impact of the Presbyterians on the expanding nation. Within three decades the population of the country doubled. Tens of thousands of new settlers arrived from Europe in a period of tremendous immigration. The removal of the Indians to their new home west of the Mississippi was followed by emigration from the South Atlantic states into the vacated territory. Expanding frontiers lured inhabitants of the eastern states and "old west" into the vast lands of the "new west" and on to the Pacific Coast. Not a few were responding to the discovery of gold in California. This movement of population led to an era of railroad-building. A brief war with Mexico ended in victory and new territory. In the South the use of the cotton gin had produced an economic revolution. Over the nation there was a spirit of optimism, troubled only by the increasing controversy over slavery.

The Old School Presbyterian Church, to which more than three fourths of the Presbyterians in the South belonged, rallied its forces to meet the challenge of the new day. The New School Church, including its congregations in the South, also sought to meet the challenge but with less success. Much of its efforts were spent in developing denominational organizations which soon appeared necessary. In 1838 the Old School Church had about one hundred twenty-five thousand members and sixteen hundred ministers. Older and wealthier congregations as well as established institutions had remained within its fold. Its center was in the Presbyterian stronghold of Pennsylvania and New Jersey. Soon its rate of growth was faster than that of the nation's population.

Home missionary activity was extended to the west coast, carried by a new generation of missionary pioneers. Foreign Mission work was increased, but Board reports were alternately filled with despair and hope. The martyrdom of eight missionaries and two children in India called forth a new dedication by the Church, and led to the choice of the first week in January as a Week of Prayer for Foreign Missions. The organization of the Church to carry out its work was further developed with the establishment of the Board of Publication in 1840 and the Board of Ministerial Relief in 1855. Relations with the New School Church continued cool, and negotiations with the Associate Reformed Presbyterian Church were fruitless. Abroad, the stand of the Free Church of Scotland for the independence of the Church was warmly supported, especially in the South. By 1860 the Old School Church was known as the largest Protestant body which was still represented in strength in both North and South; as the most conservative Church; and, according to Cyrus McCormick, as one of the two great bonds (the other was the Democratic Party) holding the Union together.

OLD SCHOOL PRESBYTERIAN CHURCH IN THE SOUTH

More than one third of the Old School Church was in the South. The Southern churches were gaining in influence. In the period between 1827 and 1861 they furnished as many Moderators of the General Assembly as during the preceding forty-eight years. Between 1844 and 1861 the Assembly held eight of its meetings south of the Mason-Dixon line. Leading Southern ministers were called to churches in the North, and Princeton Seminary sought Robert L. Dabney and Benjamin Morgan Palmer for its faculty. James Henley Thornwell, Benjamin Morgan Palmer, and Robert J. Breckinridge exercised great influence in Assembly deliberations.

Growth in the South was not spectacular but real. Emigration left some South Atlantic churches weakened and caused others to be disbanded, but the loss there was gain for the churches of the Southwest. New presbyteries and synods were organized. Texas, existing for a time as an independent country, was turned over to the Board of Foreign Missions as a field of missionary labor. Notable work was accomplished among the Indians in the Southwestern territory. R. M. Loughridge was the great apostle of the Board of Foreign Missions to the Indians, while Cyrus Kingsbury represented the American Board. Cyrus Byington labored over a grammar and translation of the Bible for the Choctaws.

Work among the Negroes was not neglected. The labors of Charles Colcock Jones of Georgia continued to be outstanding but greatest success was evident in Charleston, South Carolina. The Rev. John B. Adger had served as a missionary in Asia Minor. His life and labors there produced a remarkable work of translation, but also had resulted in much sorrow as he buried his first three children. Ill health brought him home for a rest after twelve years, and the increasing anti-slavery position of the American Board led him to feel that his services were no longer desired. For five years he labored among the Negroes of Charleston and pioneered in the erection of a building for a separate Negro congregation. His successor was one of the great preachers of the South, John L. Girardeau. Need for a larger building led to the erection of Zion Church, the largest church building in Charleston at that time. A thousand Negroes could be seated on the main floor, while the galleries were often filled with two hundred and fifty white people.

The growth of the Church resulted in an era of church building. Some of the large sanctuaries still in use were erected during this period. The First Presbyterian Church of Nashville (now the Downtown Presbyterian Church) was completed in 1851, in Egyptian style. In Richmond, Dr. Moses Drury Hoge led in the building of Second Church. The project brought from him the confession: "I go in for a stone Gothic, rubble wall, crevices for moss and ivy; holes where old Time may stick in his memorials."[1] When the building was dedicated in 1848, a hymn was written for the occasion.

Lord! thou hast said where two or three
Together come to worship thee,
Thy presence, fraught with richest grace,
Shall ever fill and bless the place.

Then let us feel, as here we raise
A temple to thy matchless praise,
The blest assurance of thy love
As it is felt in realms above.[2]

Educational and literary interests, already expressed by Presbyterians in the South, were given further attention. This was the era of the establishment of grammar schools, high schools, and colleges. Mary Baldwin College had its start in 1842 as Augusta Female Seminary. In 1849 a charter was secured for Austin College in Texas, and in 1851 Westminster College in Missouri was opened. Queens College began in 1857 as Charlotte Female Institute. A new seminary was opened in the "West." In 1853 the General Assembly authorized "an additional theological Seminary of the first class," and located Danville Theological Seminary (now Louisville Seminary) at Danville, Kentucky, the home of Centre College. Union Seminary added two new professorships. Columbia Theological Seminary, then in South Carolina, received through purchase and gift one of the largest and finest private libraries in the nation, that of Dr. Thomas Smyth.

Dr. Smyth was the author of many books. His *Ecclesiastical Republicanism* was published on both sides of the Atlantic, as were his *Presbytery and Not Prelacy* and *Unity of the Human Races*. Another noted author was William S. Plumer. His commentaries on Psalms, Romans, and Hebrews were works of sound Biblical scholarship. J. Leighton Wilson's *Western Africa* won high praise and was used by David Livingston. In the historical field the Rev. Robert Davidson contributed his *History of the Presbyterian Church in Kentucky,* and William Henry Foote produced *Sketches of North Carolina* and *Sketches of Virginia* (First and Second Series). In the field of philosophy and theology Robert J. Breckinridge wrote *Knowledge of God.* James Henley

Thornwell's contributions in philosophy, theology, and polity were collected after his death in four large volumes.

One of the most significant publications was that of *The Southern Presbyterian Review* begun in 1847. This distinguished journal was a powerful factor in the life of the Presbyterian ministers of the South, and it remains not only a testimony to the quality of thought and scholarship of the time but as an excellent source for understanding the life and thought of the Church. Dr. Robert J. Breckinridge edited *The Baltimore Literary and Religious Magazine,* followed by *The Spirit of the XIX Century.* In addition to these journals several Presbyterian weeklies exerted influence and leadership. *The Central Presbyterian* in Virginia, *The North Carolina Presbyterian, The Southern Presbyterian* in the southeastern states, and *The True Witness* in the Southwest served as sources of information and gave opportunity for expression of views.

EMPHASES OF AN INFLUENTIAL LEADER: JAMES HENLEY THORNWELL

Through these years emphases which were to characterize many of the Presbyterians of the South were given expression. The leader in bringing attention to these emphases was James Henley Thornwell. He was a South Carolinian and a symbol of the increasing influence of the "South Carolina belt" in Southern Presbyterianism. During this period South Carolina furnished the chief leaders and was the center of the intellectual life of the Church. Thornwell was the leading spirit in this development. Though he lived less than a year after the later formation of the Presbyterian Church in the Confederate States, he probably exercised more influence on that body than any other person. Educated at South Carolina College (now the University of South Carolina), Andover Seminary, and Harvard Divinity School, he became a noted teacher and scholar at South Carolina College and Columbia Seminary. His ability and influence won acknowledgment, and in 1847 at the age of thirty-four he was elected Moderator of the Old School General Assembly.

Thornwell loved the Presbyterian Church. His great concern was that the Church should express in the practical matters of organization and life the great Scriptural principles. One matter that drew his attention was the office of ruling elder. The Old School Presbyterian Church, especially in 1842-1843, was concerned with two questions. Is a ruling elder's presence necessary for a quorum of presbytery? Is it proper for a ruling elder "to lay on hands" in the ordination of a minister? Robert J. Breckinridge of Kentucky and Thornwell answered yes to both questions. The opposite view was championed by Charles Hodge. Dr. Hodge was a noted professor of Princeton Seminary, a man of gracious spirit and the leading theologian of the Old School Church. Thornwell and Hodge disagreed on the office of ruling elder. According to Thornwell, the presbyter of Scripture was a ruling elder; according to Hodge he was a preacher. Thornwell held that the ruling elder is of the same order as the minister and is in essence a clergyman; for Hodge the ruling elder represents a different order and is a layman. The view that ruling elders are necessary for a quorum of presbytery and are to "lay on hands" in the ordination of a minister was decisively rejected by the 1843 Assembly and was strongly attacked at that time even in the South. *The Watchman of the South* claimed that it was a new theory held by only a few in Southern presbyteries. Gradually Thornwell's view on quorum and ordination won acceptance until it became the position of the "Southern Presbyterian Church," which has accorded a high place to the ruling elder.

Thornwell and Hodge took opposite sides on another issue—church boards. The scene was the Assembly of 1860 in Rochester, New York. A memorable debate took place there and was continued in the religious press. One of the causes of the split of 1837 had been the position of the Old School that the Church should conduct its work through agencies under the control of the Church. So denominational boards were set up. But these boards were large; some had more than a hundred members. Honorary membership without voting privileges was granted by executive committees to those who made sizable contributions. The boards functioned to a great extent independently of the

Assembly. Had Thornwell made his stand on the evils that had arisen he might have won, for the Assembly took some corrective action. But Thornwell chose to attack the status of boards as being unscriptural. Hodge's reply was that if boards are unscriptural so are the committees supported by Thornwell, as well as all boards of trustees, etc. The Assembly supported Hodge by a vote of five to one, but at that time it also eliminated a few of the evils complained of by Thornwell. Thornwell's great emphasis was on decentralization. His ideal of small committees directly accountable to the Assembly was to become a mark of Southern Presbyterian organization.

A third emphasis which was to characterize Southern Presbyterianism received attention in this period—the spirituality of the Church. The emphasis was derived from the doctrine of the Headship of Christ. If Christ is the Head of the Church, then the Church in its organized form must confine its work to that which Christ commissioned it to do. Christ did not, said Thornwell, commission it to run the state or "reconstruct society afresh." The Church is a spiritual institution, and while the operations of the Church, in its own appropriate sphere, react upon all the interests of man, the Church, he contended, must confine itself to spiritual interests. On the basis of the spiritual function of the Church, Thornwell opposed the 1859 Assembly's endorsing the American Colonization Society, an organization transplanting liberated slaves to Liberia.

The doctrine of the spirituality of the Church was applied especially in the realm of slavery. Many Southern presbyteries and synods contended that "the relation of Master and Slave is a civil and domestic institution, and one in which no Judicatory of the Church has the right or power to legislate."[3] The Assembly had declared in 1845: "The Church of Christ is a spiritual body, whose jurisdiction extends only to the religious faith and moral conduct of her members."[4] So there was agreement that the Church is a spiritual body and restricted in its action to what is purely spiritual. But what is meant by spiritual? Hodge and many others considered Thornwell's view a new theory, restricting the realm of the Church's witness and protest only to the "religious realm of our nature." Had not Thornwell, on the basis of his theory, rejected church colleges because the Church has no business teaching "reading, writing, and ciphering"?[5] Even in the South at this time Dr. Thornwell's interpretation of spirituality was opposed. Men like Dr. B. M. Smith contended for the application of Christian principles to poverty, unemployment, etc. Thornwell's position was in part motivated by his desire to avoid the controversial political issues which would divide the Church. His emphasis on Church and State as "two distinct commonwealths," neither of which must usurp the sphere of the other, and on the nonsecularization of the Church were accepted later by "Southern Presbyterians."

On elders, boards, and spirituality of the Church, Thornwell and Hodge disagreed, but not on all matters. They served on a committee to revise the Book of Discipline, and Hodge accepted Thornwell's view that nothing ought to be considered an offense or made a matter of discipline except on the basis of Scripture. Major disagreements were but expressions of a difference in view about what Presbyterianism is. Hodge called Thornwell's position "hyper-*hyper*-HYPER-high Presbyterianism," while Thornwell named Hodge's position "no, *no*, NO Presbyterianism."[6] Their differences arose in part from their view on the use of Scripture. Thornwell held that what was not commanded in Scripture was not permissible for the Church, while Hodge held that what was not forbidden was allowable. While the principles of Hodge found greatest acceptance in the "Northern" Presbyterian Church and those of Thornwell later in the "Southern" Presbyterian Church, each of these leaders has had influence in both Churches.

TENSIONS IN CHURCH AND NATION

Debates on elders, boards, and spirituality represented attempts of the Old School Church to think through its life and mission. In the meantime there were other issues which were also disturbing the fellowship. Since 1820 slavery had been an urgent problem in the nation and was a source of increasing friction in church circles. The Assembly in its earliest years had expressed opposition to slavery and encouragement of emancipation. In 1818 the Assembly unanimously declared: "We consider the voluntary enslaving of one part of the human race by another as a gross violation of the most precious and sacred rights of human nature, as utterly inconsistent with the law of God . . . and as totally irreconcilable with the spirit and the principles of the Gospel of Christ."[7] The dangers of immediate emancipation were admitted, but Presbyterians were exhorted to work for the "total abolition of slavery." In spite of the deliverance of 1818, slaveholding had never been interpreted as a bar to church membership. But Southern presbyteries became increasingly unhappy over the 1818 deliverance. In 1836 twelve of them overtured the Assembly, unsuccessfully, that it should be rescinded. At this time there began a trend to avoid controversy on the slavery issue. The 1845 Old School Assembly declared that slaveholding was not forbidden in Scripture and, therefore, was not in all circumstances wrong, that it was not a bar to Christian communion, and that the Church had "no authority to legislate on the subject."[8] When objections to this declaration were raised, the 1846 Assembly stated that it had always held the same position.

The increasing attention to slavery was a product of the new importance of slavery to the cotton economy of the South and a response to the abolition movement which, though small, was vocal and fanatic. All slaveholding is sinful, the abolitionists said; all slaveholders must be barred from membership in the Church; all slaves must be immediately freed. In defense Southerners took up the pen. Among the ablest defenders of slavery were Southern Presbyterians. While there is evidence that many Southern Presbyterian ministers did not approve of slavery, some of them wrote to show that it was a "positive good." It was not contrary to Scripture or the spirit of the gospel; it was not a violation of the rights of men. It was "necessary, just, and a good relation." Dependence and servitude fitted the Negro character and was God's providential arrangement for the Negro's greatest good. So reasoned Dr. Thornwell. Dr. Benjamin Morgan Palmer, pastor of the First Presbyterian Church of New Orleans, drew what he considered to be the inevitable conclusion, "The plain duty" of Southern people is that of "conserving and transmitting the system of slavery."[9]

The slavery controversy increased the growing tension in the nation. North and South differed socially, economically, and politically. In 1830 and 1850 secession was favored by a large number in South Carolina. There was also much discontent elsewhere, especially in 1850. But love for the Union triumphed, aided by Presbyterians in the South. Thornwell wrote: "I was not a Nullifier in South Carolina and could not have been a Repudiator in Mississippi. . . . The prospect of disunion is one which I cannot contemplate without absolute horror. . . . God grant that our country may be saved."[10] In Virginia, Robert L. Dabney and Moses Drury Hoge were still Union men early in 1861. The secession of South Carolina aroused Dabney. "As for South Carolina," he wrote, "the little impudent vixen has gone beyond all patience."[11] His "Pacific Appeal to Christians," issued on the eve of the War Between the States, was a plea for patience and moderation and for the preservation of the Union.

Defense of the Union in the South at this time was a lost cause. The election of Lincoln, "a sectional candidate," was, according to Thornwell, "the straw that has broken the camel's back."[12] After this, most of the Southern Presbyterians supported the secession movement. Thornwell said, "The sooner it is brought about the better." The most famous stand was that of Dr. Palmer. In a two-hour Thanksgiving sermon, November 29, 1860, he sounded the call for "southern rights" and of the duty "which patriotism and religion alike require of us all. . . . This spirit of atheism [abolition], which knows no God who tolerates evil, no Bible which sanctions law . . . has selected us for its victims and slavery as its issue." Palmer found Lincoln to be "nearly as impotent for good as he is competent for evil." "To the South the high position is assigned of defending, before all nations, the cause of all religion and of all truth. . . . Not till the last man has fallen behind the last rampart shall it [our trust] drop from our hands. . . . Let the people of all the Southern States, in solemn council assembled, reclaim the powers they have delegated. Let them . . . take all the necessary steps looking to separate and independent existence."[13] On the same day the Synod of South Carolina declared: "The Synod has no hesitation, therefore, in expressing the belief that the people of South Carolina are now solemnly called on to imitate their revolutionary forefathers, and stand up for their rights. . . . We, Ministers and Elders of the Presbyterian Church in South Carolina, in Synod assembled, would give them our benediction . . ."[14]

Revolution in the life of the nation did not leave unaffected the life of the Church. The slavery controversy had led to bitter fights in denominations and had caused divisions. Through the period the growing sectional consciousness had been reflected in church circles. Presbyterians in the South had long been aware of their distance from the main centers of Presbyterian strength in Pennsylvania and New Jersey. Further, it seemed to them that much of the denominational effort had been expended in the North and West rather than in the Southern states. A feeling that the South was neglected was accompanied by a growing belief that the South was a unified section with its own problems and needs. The founding of the seminaries in Hampden-Sydney and Columbia was a reflection of sectional feeling and a determination not to depend on "unfriendly regions" for ministers. The establishment of the Southern Board of Missions in South Carolina in 1833, and of the Southwestern Advisory Committee of the Board of Domestic Missions in New Orleans in 1859 are evidences of a Southern Presbyterian mind-set. There are many references in sermons and writings to "our Southern Zion," "our Southern Church," and "the Southern Presbyterian Church." The consciousness of a Southern Presbyterianism was especially strong in the "South Carolina belt." The Synod of South Carolina, in 1837 and 1860, debated overtures calling for the organization of a separate Church.

Anti-slavery agitation in the Old School Church increased the tensions between the Northern and Southern sections of the Church. The fact that the 1860 Assembly was harmonious was a surprise to many. But the South believed that she still had many friends in the Northern churches. This belief was greatly shaken in January, 1861. *The Princeton Review* carried an article by its editor, Charles Hodge, on the state of the country. Dr. Hodge wrote to show that the complaints of the South were either unfounded or not just cause for secession. What wrongs the South had suffered had been committed by the abolitionists. These extremists should be blamed, not the whole North. Hodge said his article was written in the interest of peace, but it met almost universal condemnation among the hundreds of Southern Presbyterian readers. Hodge the great friend now turned enemy! What hope was there if Charles Hodge had now joined the anti-slavery cause? Many of the Presbyterians in the South began to doubt that Northern and Southern Presbyterians could be happy in one Church. *The Southern Presbyterian* carried an editorial in its issue of March 16, 1861. "We believe, therefore, that it will be ultimately found desirable and proper for the Presbyterian Church in the Confederate States to be completely organized separately and independently from the Presbyterian Church in the United States." But some letters to the editor maintained that a church division in the midst of political separation would impair the testimony to the independence of the Church.

THE CRUCIAL 1861 ASSEMBLY

The General Assembly of the Old School Church convened May 16, 1861, in Philadelphia. The period was one of great excitement. Ten states had seceded; Fort Sumter had fallen; Lincoln had called for volunteers. Philadelphia newspapers reported troop movements and carried articles on the Old School Assembly, with repeated demands for a strong expression by that Church in support of the Union. When the Assembly opened, the galleries were packed with interested spectators. Patriotism was in the air.

The Assembly was smaller than that of the previous years. Out of sixty-four Southern presbyteries, thirty-three were not represented. Apart from the presbyteries in the border Synods of Baltimore, Kentucky, Missouri, and Upper Missouri, only thirteen Southern presbyteries were represented by sixteen commissioners. There was not a single delegate from any presbytery in North Carolina, South Carolina, Georgia, Alabama, and Arkansas. One of six Virginia presbyteries was represented, but Mississippi had commissioners from six of seven presbyteries. Some presbyteries had declined to elect commissioners because the war was on. Other presbyteries chose commissioners but later rescinded the action in view of personal danger. The representatives from Concord Presbytery declined to attend because of the "blockade" and the failure of the committee on arrangements to answer their letters. Other commissioners were absent, it appears, with deliberate purpose. The Mississippi presbyteries reported that they were "insulted" for being represented at Philadelphia and that John B. Adger, a leading minister of South Carolina, had written that Southern men had no business to be in any such Assembly. Thornwell, the great leader of the Southern Presbyterians, was absent. He sent a message to the Assembly expressing the hope that God would restore harmony and good will between his country and theirs!

There appeared to be a determination to keep the political issue out of the Assembly. The opening sermon was on the text "My kingdom is not of this world." But the emotional patriotism, packed galleries, newspaper columns, and letters from home had their influence. Dr. Gardiner Spring, pastor of the large Brick Presbyterian Church of New York City, introduced resolutions asking the Assembly to call on its churches and ministers to do all in their power to "strengthen, uphold, and encourage the Federal government."[15] Those who thought such a deliverance was not the business of the Church succeeded in delaying the passing of the resolutions during many days of debate. Finally, the Assembly succumbed. Rejecting a majority report of eight members of a committee of nine, the Assembly supported a minority report offered by one member! Dr. Charles Hodge and fifty-seven others protested this "political deliverance" which gave needless hurt to the South, but to no avail. The protest served only to keep the border synods in the Old School Church.

PLANS FOR A SOUTHERN PRESBYTERIAN CHURCH

The reaction of the Presbyterians in the South was soon evident. Dr. John N. Waddell, minister and educator of Tennessee, addressed an open letter to Dr. Spring. "At a time when the whole land was in a state of revolution, when there had been in existence for months two distinct governments, to each of which their respective citizens felt bound to render their obedience; when, if ever, there was a time for the exercise of forbearance, this was the time; when very few southern commissioners were present; when it was or might have been supposed that they were loyal to their own section; when there was in point of fact, no need for the expression of any opinion, or the utterance of any voice, in one way or another, in regard to the state of the country . . . then it was, at such a time, under such circumstances, that Dr. Spring, venerable Patriarch of the Brick Church, conceived himself called upon to bring forward . . . a set of resolutions of the most incendiary nature . . ."[16]

The Gardiner Spring resolutions were not considered the cause of the division of the Old School Church; but they were given as the reason such a division was not made peacefully, without "conflict of feeling," and why the division was continued after the war was over. However, they were described by the Synod of Kentucky as the "chief pretext" for schism. Presbyterian leaders in the South declared that a separation would have been necessary in view of the existence of two separate nations. Still the resolutions were viewed as an important factor. The Southern presbyteries and synods during the summer and fall of 1861 ended their connections with the Old School Assembly and cited the political character of the resolutions. Objection to the resolutions was not because the Assembly had urged support of government but because the Assembly decided a political question. The

Southern interpretation of the Constitution was that primary allegiance was due to the states, while the Northern interpretation was that primary allegiance was due the central government. As a church court the Assembly had no right to decide that the latter interpretation was right. Further, the resolutions were viewed as putting in an impossible situation all commissioners from states that had withdrawn from the Union. They were forced to choose between allegiance to their state or allegiance to the declaration of the Church. They felt that Southern members were "virtually" forced out of the Church. This action of the Assembly was made under trying circumstances. Dr. Benjamin Morgan Palmer later declared, "We do not undertake even to say that, with our positions reversed and acting under their convictions, we might not have been guilty of the same fault." [17] But fault it was considered. The Church took action on a "strictly political issue."

The movement for a Southern Church met enthusiastic response. Church papers in the South took a leading role in urging separation and keeping the churches informed. A circular in Virginia called for a convention in Richmond to take appropriate action. The Presbytery of Orange in North Carolina favored a convention in Augusta, Georgia; East Alabama Presbytery voted for Columbia, South Carolina. Greensboro, Raleigh, and Charlotte, in North Carolina, and Memphis, Tennessee, were also suggested. The Convention to be held "while the Presbyteries are all harmonious" [18] was to make plans for a "provisional government" until a constitution was adopted. The idea of a convention was opposed by some as having no place in Presbyterian government, while others did not like the proposed locations determined by "the convenience of the seaboard." Meanwhile, presbytery after presbytery severed connection with the Assembly. Similar action was taken by the synods in the fall. In June a group of South Carolina ministers sent an address to the Presbyterian churches of the South on the subject of Foreign Missions. Churches were refusing to send funds to the New York office. The ministers suggested that all contributions be sent to Dr. J.

Leighton Wilson, who had resigned as one of the secretaries of the Board of Foreign Missions. These funds were to be used for the support of Southern Presbyterians on the foreign field and for Indian work. The Southwestern Advisory Committee of the Board of Domestic Missions collected funds for home missions.

The Convention met in Atlanta in August, 1861. "Eleven of the forty-five presbyteries" (the presbyteries in the border states had not withdrawn from the Assembly) were represented. Plans were made for a General Assembly in Augusta, Georgia, in December. Advice was sent to presbyteries on steps to be taken lest "the right of succession in law, and corresponding interests be endangered." Special attention was given to foreign missions. The convention closed with a declaration on the war. ". . . it would say to all within the compass of it, 'up, quit you like men, be strong.' Put your treasures in the lap of your Country; throw your stout arms about her . . . if need be let your blood flow like water . . . Put your trust in God and pray your Country through this dreadful War." [19] The Convention adjourned. All eyes turned to Augusta, Georgia. It was a place "central, retired," and "near to South Carolina." There the first Assembly of the Southern Church was to be held.

The Presbyterian Church in the Confederate States

THE FIRST ASSEMBLY of the Presbyterians in the South was convened at Augusta, Georgia, December 4, 1861. Fifty ministers and thirty-eight elders, with an average age of over fifty years, were enrolled from forty-seven presbyteries (two presbyteries from the Synod of Baltimore having joined the forty-five of the South). These commissioners represented almost eleven hundred churches and seventy-five thousand members. A new Church was being born, but one rooted in the heritage of the past. Old ties were broken, with mixed feeling. If these Southern Presbyterians did not recall the Gardiner Spring resolutions in anger, they, in no mood to consider the circumstances, remembered with righteous indignation the "political deliverance" of the Philadelphia Assembly. But there was some sadness. "[Our separation] argues no breach of charity, and therefore implies no schism," wrote Dr. Thornwell in a Valedictory Letter to the Presbyterian Church in the United States of America. "Your Faith and Order are ours. Your noble testimony for the truth in by-gone days is still ours. All that is precious in the past is still ours; and we sincerely pray, that the two Churches may hereafter have no other rivalry but that of love to the Master, and of holy zeal in His cause. We bid you Farewell!"[1] Dr. Thornwell wanted to send the letter in the name of the new Assembly but objections were raised and the message was never dispatched.

The new body, adopting the name of the Presbyterian Church in the Confederate States, had much to do, and would accomplish creative results before this meeting was over. But the beginning was with the past. The commissioners approved the appointing of "the Standing Committees which are usual in the

General Assembly of the Presbyterian Church in the United States," and decided that "this Assembly shall be governed by the rules and precedents of the Presbyterian Church in the United States, until otherwise ordered." They declared that "the Confession of Faith, the Larger and Shorter Catechisms, the Form of Government, the Book of Discipline, and the Directory of Worship, which together make up the Constitution of the Presbyterian Church in the United States of America, are the Constitution of the Presbyterian Church in the Confederate States,"[2] and made plans to use the Psalms and hymns approved by the mother Church.

IMPORTANT DOCUMENTS OF THE
FIRST SOUTHERN ASSEMBLY

Three important documents came out of this first Assembly. Because they are among the classic statements of the Southern Church and provide an introduction to its thought, some passages are chosen for quotation. The first document was the opening sermon, printed in the appendix to the Minutes. The preacher, Benjamin Morgan Palmer, was chosen for the task by the Assembly, but, having been nominated previously by the Convention in Atlanta, he came prepared. There was much to commend him for the position. His ministry in Savannah, Columbia, and New Orleans had established him as one of the great preachers of America. Hardly less outstanding was his service as a pastor. Death had visited his immediate family often. Probably out of the comfort he received in sorrow came his qualification for a ministry of sympathy and comfort, extended "house by house" and through an extensive correspondence. In his letters he almost without fail paused to ask, "How are you speeding in your Christian course?" No one could doubt that he loved the South and the new Confederacy. He was a slaveholder, a passionate defender of the Southern view of slavery, and an ardent secessionist. In full strength and vigor, his "medium stature and slender frame" showed little evidence of his forty-three years. It was this man who was chosen to deliver the sermon and was later elected Moderator.

Dr. Palmer ascended the pulpit in the First Presbyterian Church of Augusta on the morning of December 4. His text was Ephesians 1:22, 23, and his theme "The Supreme Dominion to Which Christ Is Exalted as Head of the Church, and the Glory of the Church in that Relation, as Being at Once His Body and His Fullness." The magnificent sermon was Scriptural and filled with Scripture, clearly outlined and with orderly progression. After the war Dr. Palmer declared that if he had been guilty of mentioning political themes in the pulpit, he would not do so again. He touched on no political themes on this occasion, and made only the briefest allusion to the current situation. Occasionally he referred to "this infant nation." Once he mentioned what happened in the Philadelphia Assembly. "But a little while since, it was attempted in the most august court of our Church to place the crown of Our Lord upon the head of Caesar—to bind that body, which is Christ's fulness, to the chariot in which that Caesar rides." His subject now was Christ and the Church. "Through the unfolding ages she has moved securely on, while disastrous change has ground to powder and scattered to the winds the proudest dynasties of earth. Kings have bound her with fetters of brass; but the fair captive has taken again her harp from the willows, and God has made her walls salvation and her gates praise. Amidst the fires of martyrdom, she has risen younger from the ashes of her own funeral pile. Wooing the nations with her accents of love, she lengthens her cords to gather them into her broad pavilion. And when the whole frame of nature shall be dissolved, she will stand serene above the burning earth, to welcome her descending Lord. Caught up by Him into the heavens, she will gather into her communion there all the elder sons of God; still the immortal Church of the Redeemer, out-living all time and henceforth counting her years upon the dial of eternity! . . .

"Brethren, we have to-day been gazing into heaven after our ascending Lord, ascending to His Headship and His Crown.

From His gracious throne He unfolds the sacred parchment on which our charter and commission are engrossed: 'Go ye into all the world and disciple all nations!' With pathetic gesture, He also points over mountains, continents and seas to the 'other sheep which are not of this fold,' wandering upon the bleak heather, under the dark star of some idol god. May the rushing mighty wind of the Pentecostal day fill this house where we are sitting! and may the tongue of fire rest upon each of this Assembly! . . . Sinking personal ambition, and forgetful of sectional aggrandizement, let us strive to equip the Church with the necessary agencies for the prosecution of her solemn work. Let us build her towers and establish her bulwarks just where the most effective assaults may be made upon the Kingdoms of Satan; that 'her righteousness may go forth as brightness, and her salvation as a lamp that burneth;' and Zion become 'a crown of glory,' 'a royal diadem in the hand of our God.'" No wonder it was later said of Dr. Palmer, "He preaches like an archangel!"

Another notable document of this first Assembly was "An Address to All the Churches of Jesus Christ." Prepared by a committee under the leadership of Dr. Thornwell, the address was carefully studied by the Assembly as it was read and reread. On the eleventh day, December 14, in connection with the regular roll call, the members of the Assembly came forward and signed the document as it lay on the Moderator's table. Memories went back to glorious days in Scotland when Presbyterians signed their national covenants. "In thus taking its place among sister Churches of this and other countries, it seems proper that it should set forth the causes which have impelled it to separate from the Church of the North, and to indicate a general view of the course which it feels it incumbent upon it to pursue in the new circumstances in which it is placed. . . . We are not conscious of any purpose to rend the body of Christ. . . . we have been prompted by a sincere desire to promote the glory of God, and the efficiency, energy, harmony and zeal of His visible Kingdom in the earth. . . . we are persuaded that the interests of true religion will be more effectually subserved by two independent Churches, under the circumstances in which two countries are placed, than by one united body ... if we should remain together, the political questions which divide us as citizens, will be obtruded on our Church Courts, and discussed by Christian Ministers and Elders with all the acrimony, bitterness and rancour with which such questions are usually discussed by men of the world."

In setting forth the spirituality of the Church, the cardinal emphasis of this first Assembly, attention was called to the distinct provinces of Church and State. "The State is a natural institute . . . It is the society of rights. The Church is a supernatural institute . . . It is the society of the redeemed. The State aims at social order, the Church at spiritual holiness. The State looks to the visible and outward, the Church is concerned for the invisible and inward . . . The power of the Church is exclusively spiritual, that of the State includes the exercise of force . . . The Church has no right to construct or modify a government for the State, and the State has no right to frame a creed or polity for the Church."

Reasons for the separation from the Old School Church were reviewed. The unconstitutionality of the proceedings in the Philadelphia Assembly, it was affirmed, were not in themselves sufficient ground for division. But those procedures opened the door for "the introduction of the worst passions of human nature into the deliberations of Church Courts." The independent organization of the Southern Church could be "scripturally maintained" on another ground. "The unity of the Church does not require a formal bond of union among all the congregations of believers throughout the earth." As the unity of the human race is not disturbed by its divisions into countries, so the "unity of the spiritual seed of Christ is neither broken nor impaired by separation and division into various Church Constitutions." It appeared desirable, therefore, especially under the circumstances, "that Churches should be bounded by national lines." In spite of the high tone of the argument, occasionally a note of pride is found: "We have never confounded Caesar and Christ."

It was not that these Southern Presbyterians had ceased to love the Church of their fathers—"not that they have adjured its ancient principles, or forgotten its glorious history. It is to give these same principles a richer, freer, fuller development among ourselves than they possibly could receive under foreign culture. It is precisely because we love that Church as it was, and that Church as it should be, that we have resolved, as far as in us lies, to realize its grand idea in the country, and under the Government where God has cast our lot."

Affirming that "in our ecclesiastical capacity, we are neither the friends nor the foes of slavery," commissioners, the majority of whom were slaveholders, set forth and defended the Southern position on slavery. Since they had been maligned among the Churches abroad on this subject, they explained their views in full, and added, "We have concealed nothing." They were frank to admit that "without [slavery] we are profoundly persuaded that the African race in the midst of us can never be elevated in the scale of being." Their conservatism was shown in their view of the Negro's human rights, "It must be shown that the minimum which falls to his lot at the bottom of the line is out of proportion to his capacity and culture." They stood, they said, "upon the foundation of the Prophets and Apostles, Jesus Christ Himself being the chief cornerstone." "Others, if they please, may spend their time in declaiming on the tyranny of earthly masters; it will be our aim to resist the real tyrants which oppress the soul—Sin and Satan."

The address concluded with a statement of the goals of the new Church. "The ends which we propose to accomplish as a Church are the same as those which are proposed by every other Church. To proclaim God's truth as a witness to the nations; to gather His elect from the four corners of the earth, and through the Word, Ministries, and Ordinances to train them for eternal life, is the great business of His people. The only thing that will be at all peculiar to us, is the manner in which we shall attempt to discharge our duty." Forsaking the usual custom of resorting to societies more or less closely connected with the Church, "It is our purpose to rely upon the regular organs of our government, and executive agencies directly and immediately responsible to them. . . . we shall, therefore, endeavor to do what has never yet been adequately done—bring out the energies of our Presbyterian system of government."

A third great document of the Assembly was given expression in the course of setting up the organization of the Church. Boards were dispensed with, and the work of the Church was to be carried on through executive committees chosen by, dependent upon, and responsible to the Assembly. The aim was the complete subordination of every agency to the Assembly, so that no agency could have independent authority. The ideal was the Church its own missionary society, the Church its own educational society. Executive committees were set up for Foreign Missions, Domestic Missions, Education, and Publication. The committees were in reality commissions acting for the Assembly between meetings of that body. In connection with Foreign Missions, there was the declaration of intent to be a missionary Church. "Finally, the General Assembly desires distinctly and deliberately to inscribe on our Church's banner, as she now first unfurls it to the world, in immediate connection with the Headship of her Lord, His last command: 'Go ye into all the world and preach the gospel to every creature': regarding this as the great end of her organization, and obedience to it as the indispensable condition of her Lord's promised presence, and as one great comprehensive object a proper conception of whose vast magnitude and grandeur is the only thing which in connection with the love of Christ can sufficiently arouse her energies and develop her resources, so as to cause her to carry on with the vigor and efficiency which true fealty to her Lord demands, those other agencies necessary to her internal growth and home prosperity."

SHARING IN SUFFERING

The commissioners did not forget that they were a part of a new nation. The minutes of the Assembly read, "Saturday morning, December 7, 9½ o'clock. The Assembly met and spent the first half hour in special prayer for the blessing of God upon the cause of the Confederate States, according to previous order." For all their condemnation of the acts of their Northern brethren, and in spite of earnest effort, some secular and political matters crept into their minutes. Thornwell, the apostle of the spirituality of the Church, overtured the Assembly to ask the Confederate government to recognize Christianity as its official religion, but the Assembly would not approve and the overture was withdrawn. The Confederacy was the native land and the accepted government of these Southern Presbyterians. Already they were pouring out their wealth for her. Many were to give their sons for her cause. They interpreted their victories as "the marked interpositions of God in our favor" and saw their defeats as "His chastisements for our sins."[3] They believed God was on their side. "Our cause is preeminently the cause of God himself and every blow struck by us is in defense of his supremacy," affirmed Dr. Palmer. So they were confident that God would not let their enemies triumph. In the final defeats of the spring of 1865, Harmony Presbytery was still "fondly anticipating and expecting the day when God will put down our haughty and wicked foes." Through the years they prayed, in the words of the Synod of North Carolina, that "the Lord God may be a wall of fire around our land; that the Angel of the Covenant may go forth as the Captain of our hosts; that the Holy Ghost may pour out upon our people a spirit of grace and supplication that we may be a people exalted by righteousness . . ." They prayed for "the President of the Confederacy and his counsellors—the Generals, officers and soldiers of our armies . . . for the bereaved widows and orphans of our murdered brethren, and that the Lord may send us peace in His own time, and that He may overrule all these calamities for His own glory . . ."[4]

What calamities there were! Harmony Presbytery came to its spring meeting in 1865 "with the wail of lamentation and sorrow. She hangs her harps upon the willows and weeps as she remembers Zion."[5] At that time the South was all but destroyed, a large portion of her territory overrun. The war had taken an awful toll of her men. Wealth was gone. Homes were plundered. Families were destitute.

In all of this suffering the churches shared. The 1862 Assembly, with only twenty-five presbyteries represented, met in Montgomery instead of Memphis because of the Confederate disaster at the battle of Shiloh. In 1863 the Assembly received the news of the death of the Presbyterian general, "Stonewall" Jackson, and missed the counsel of Dr. Thornwell who had died in August of 1862. The Synod of Nashville was unable to have a meeting from 1861 to 1866; and the Presbytery of New Orleans was forced, because of the capture of the city, to meet in two sections during the war years. Columbia Seminary had lost Thornwell, and shared in the poverty and devastation left after General Sherman's visit, though the seminary buildings were not burned. Its professors were paid in coupons and provisions. Union Seminary had two students in 1862-1863, and three in 1863-1864, and at the end of the war a faculty without salary. Danville Seminary was wrecked, but not completely. Most of the colleges suspended operations. The difficulty of securing paper drove most church periodicals out of business. A hundred sanctuaries were destroyed or heavily damaged and others were turned into hospitals or storehouses. Congregations were broken up. In Charleston, the large Second Church saw its congregation "gradually reduced to a mere handful." No regular meeting of the session could be held for four years. The Second Church, Memphis, was seized by the Federal authorities on the grounds that its members were disloyal to the government of the United States. The church bell had been offered to the Confederate government to be molded into cannon.

A part of the suffering lay in separations. With the capture of New Orleans in 1862, Benjamin Morgan Palmer, who had left the city, was kept apart from the church he served until July, 1865. The great love of pastor and people made the experience trying. In 1864 Palmer wrote his people, ". . . I transfer myself [in mind] to the dear old pulpit, which I had learned to reverence, as a king his throne. It has required little imagination to people the pews with their old occupants; and thus to reproduce, one by one, the families of my own happy charge, just as they were accustomed to sit down the long-drawn aisles of that grand and beautiful sanctuary. The dear children of the flock were [pictured] before me, exactly as I was wont to see them gathered into classes in the Sabbath-school. When weary of the large assembly, it needed only the waving of the wand to remand all to their several homes: and I would find myself now treading the familiar streets of our city, house after house rising up before the mind just as of yore when my hand was upon each door bell." [6]

Through all the calamities the Church sought to serve. Moses Drury Hoge in the capital of the Confederacy reported "six sermons a week, and funerals extra . . . with pastoral visits thrown in . . . but this is only the beginning . . . A discharged soldier . . . writes to me to get his pay; a wife, separated from her husband, writes, begging me to get her a permit . . . to go to him; an exile, driven by the enemy from his home, writes, asking if I can assist him in getting a position where he can make bread for his destitute family . . ." [7] In addition to usual duties, the pastors spent much time in preaching tours to army units.

THE CHURCH'S MINISTRY TO
CONFEDERATE SOLDIERS

The Church followed the troops to camp and to battle. The 1862 Assembly asked that special prayer be offered in the churches on the last Sabbath of every month for "our baptized young men in the army." In a pastoral letter to its members in uniform the Assembly said, "Whether you are officers, soldiers, or chaplains, remember in every case that you are ambassadors for God . . ." [8] The Committee on Domestic Missions was given responsibility for seeing that the spiritual needs of the armed forces were met. While home mission activities of the committee were barely supported during war years, there was a generous response to provide for the men in uniform. The committee encouraged pastors to preach to units near them and to visit units from their locality. Regular chaplains were used, and their inadequate army pay was supplemented by the Church. In addition to pastors giving part time to preaching in the camps, the Church maintained missionaries. These missionaries gave full time to their labors among the soldiers, but their location and work were under the control of the Church instead of the army. The goal of the Committee of Domestic Missions was a chaplain or missionary in every Confederate brigade and laborers for the hospitals. In 1864 there were one hundred thirty ministers in the army, about one fifth of the total ministerial force. The committee also used the plan of appointing commissioners to the main divisions of the army. The commissioner served as a chaplain, helped secure chaplains, aided in obtaining acceptance and use of chaplains by the army, and sought to introduce some system into the work in their area. Among the commissioners, John N. Waddell served the Army of Mississippi, William Flinn was with the Army of Tennessee, and B. T. Lacy with the Army of Northern Virginia.

One of the services of the Church was to provide tracts and Bibles. The Committee on Publication distributed "A Call to Prayer," "The Wounded, or A Time to Think," "Death of a Christian Soldier," and many others. *The Soldier's Visitor,* with a circulation of eight thousand, was offered free to all Presbyterian soldiers. Fifteen thousand copies of an army hymnbook were printed. *The Christian Observer,* although not an official Church publication, was one of the favorite pieces of reading matter among the Presbyterians. Three thousand free copies were distributed each week to the Confederate Army.

The need for Bibles became acute in spite of the work of the American Bible Society and the Confederate Bible Society. Dr. Moses Drury Hoge of Richmond planned an appeal to the Christians of Great Britain. Convinced that a personal visit would be more fruitful, he ran the blockade and returned with fifteen thousand Bibles, fifty thousand New Testaments, two hundred and fifty thousand Gospels and Psalms, as well as a large amount of other religious books and tracts. His service won the commendation of his Synod and the Committee of Publication and a letter of gratitude from General Lee.

Worship services in the camps were not in ideal surroundings. Robert L. Dabney, chaplain in 1861 and chief of staff to "Stonewall" Jackson in 1862, wrote of his experiences: "Overhead there is no roof besides the azure of heaven. The place of worship is nothing but an oblong area between two rows of tents, and a pulpit is a rude box to elevate the minister a step from the earth . . . on either hand are clusters of glittering arms stacked, soldiers reclining on their pallets, and the open doors of tents, filled with their occupants."[9] Later, in other places, little crude chapels were built.

Among the experiences of Presbyterian chaplains recorded in diaries and journals is that of W. S. Lacy, who was in the front lines in 1864. His men were singing the Doxology. "As the voices swelled and rolled heavenward, with rich volume, like soft thunder, lo! in the distance we could hear the echo—or, was it the echo? As the men hushed with expectancy, waiting for the benediction, we heard from the camp of the enemy the same magnificent and matchless melody. Captain Langford . . . said, 'Chaplain, let us join in,' and again from the dark recess behind temporary earthworks, our men took up the grand refrain, and Northern and Southern soldier joined in singing—as has been done many a day since—

> Praise God, from whom all blessings flow;
> Praise Him, all creatures here below;
> Praise Him above, ye heavenly host;
> Praise Father, Son, and Holy Ghost."[10]

The work of the Church for the soldiers was not without result. Presbyterians shared in the great revival that took place in the Confederate Army. The years 1863 and 1864 appear to have been the most fruitful period. Chief results were in Virginia, where first-fruits were mentioned by the 1862 Assembly. The Synod of Virginia in 1863 noted the "extraordinary outpouring of the Holy Spirit upon our Army during the past year."[11] Revival spread to the army of General Longstreet, the army of North Georgia, the army of Mississippi, and to units west of the Mississippi, as well as in other areas. The 1864 Assembly heard with gratitude of "the wonderful work of grace in our Armies," and that there had probably been over twelve thousand conversions that year. It is estimated that over one hundred thousand Confederate soldiers were converted during the war years. Some of these entered seminary after the war and became leading ministers in the Southern Church.

SERVICE TO NEGROES AND INDIANS

There were other groups requiring the ministry of the Church. East Alabama Presbytery reported: "That class of persons which has contributed so much to enkindle the wrath of our enemies against us, receives the special attention of almost every pastor . . . the same lips that proclaim good tidings to the Master, are heard . . . holding forth the same salvation to the servant."[12] The 1861 Assembly heard a report on work among the Negroes from the aged Dr. Charles Colcock Jones. He urged pastors "as a good shepherd" to "follow them into the highways and hedges, into their plantations and into their own sick chambers . . . attend their funerals, and follow them to their graves."[13] It was reported to the Assembly in 1863 that more work was being done for the Negroes than in any previous period, and in several presbyteries there were reports of a "quiet but increasing revival" among them.

Indians early became objects of concern for the Southern Church. Their desperate need commended them, and their Southern sympathies were welcomed. Dr. J. Leighton Wilson visited the tribes in the fall of 1861. Two noted missionaries were present at the first Assembly as commissioners, representing Creek Nation Presbytery and Indian Presbytery, both in the Synod of Arkansas. The Assembly accepted responsibility for the Indian work within its bounds and approved of the sending of six new missionaries. But the fortunes of war prevented the carrying out of this plan. Indian territory itself became a battleground. The result during war years was loss rather than gain.

Work among the Indians was carried on by the Committee of Foreign Missions, which also maintained contact with and sent contributions to the few Southern Presbyterians serving in the foreign field. The Secretary of this Committee was Dr. J. Leighton Wilson. Dr. Wilson had spent almost twenty years as a missionary in Africa and eight years as one of the Secretaries of the Presbyterian Board of Foreign Missions in New York. When war began he cast his lot with the South. His work before and during the first Assembly was chiefly responsible for the Southern Church's acceptance of its missionary calling. Dr. Wilson was the first Secretary of the Committee of Foreign Missions and in 1863 assumed also the responsibilities as Secretary of Domestic Missions. It was he who planned and worked out the great program for ministering to the men in uniform, and who bore the burden of the destitute home mission churches during the final two years of war. Not only was Dr. Wilson an able man. His character won from Dr. Charles Hodge the confession that Dr. Wilson had more of the apostolic spirit than anyone else he ever knew, and from Dr. Robert L. Dabney the testimony that everyone was certain of the purity of Dr. Wilson's aims. These estimates help to explain why the Church was ready to accept his leadership and responded to his proposals.

FRIENDLY RELATIONS AND UNIONS WITH OTHER CHURCHES

The General Assembly was able to meet each year during the war, although in 1862 the place of meeting had to be changed, and in 1865 the Assembly met in December instead of May. One of the concerns of the Assembly through these years was its relations with other churches. The Address to All the Churches in 1861 had been an expression of this interest. The ties with the Northern Church were ended, but, apart from the charge of the political activity of the 1861 Northern Assembly, no harsh words appear in the minutes with respect to that body. Charges of treason and rebellion made against the South by the Northern Assembly in 1862 and other years brought no accusations against the

Northern Church, but there are many references in Southern Church courts to "our cruel and malignant enemy." The first Assembly solicited fraternal correspondence with "Churches of like faith and order in the Confederate States of America." Among the groups named were the Associate Reformed Presbyterian Church, the Independent Presbyterian Church, the Cumberland Presbyterian Church, and the United Synod of the South. Union with the Associate Reformed Presbyterians was solicited in 1861 but declined by that group. The Southern Church was also anxious to bring the Cumberland Church to a merger but had no success. The Independent Presbyterian Church was composed of eleven churches in South and North Carolina. Union with this group followed approval of the 1863 Assembly and the subsequent action of the Synod of South Carolina. "Heresies" which had led to the foundation of that Church half a century earlier had passed away. The United Synod of the South was composed of New School churches in the South which had separated from the New School Assembly in 1857 because of anti-slavery deliverances. This synod had fifteen presbyteries, two hundred churches, and twelve thousand members. The movement for union was led by Presbyterians in Virginia. There were only a few who had fears that these New School churches were still "new school" in their theology. A common view on slavery and common involvement in the Southern cause were influential factors. Robert L. Dabney, who led the Southern Presbyterian negotiations, was also interested in preventing the establishment by the United Synod of a seminary in Virginia. Opposition to this union was led by Dr. John B. Adger and Dr. Palmer. By an overwhelming vote the presbyteries of the United Synod were received into the Southern Church on the basis of the doctrinal position of the Southern Church.

The increase gained through the regular nurture of the Church, the revivals, and the unions were the beginning of rapid growth. This new strength would be needed as the Church faced the postwar task.

CHAPTER V

Desolations Repaired

THE SPRING OF 1865 was a time of disaster for the South. Her capital fell, her armies surrendered, and her territory was plundered. No meeting of the General Assembly could be held in May amid "the extremely agitated state of the country" and "the rapid rushing of events." It was not until December, with the war over and the Confederacy dissolved, that the "violent revolution" had subsided sufficiently to permit the gathering. In those tragic days, when the poverty and oppression of Reconstruction were beginning, the Assembly convened in Macon, Georgia. The retiring Moderator, Dr. John S. Wilson, preached the opening sermon from Joshua 13:1, "There remaineth yet very much land to be possessed."

Though the nation was once again united, there was little disposition to end the independent organization of the Southern Church. The Synod of Virginia, meeting in October, found it "incumbent on us to maintain our ecclesiastical lines unbroken, and to go forward in the path to which the Providence of God has summoned us."[1] Harmony Presbytery saw "no good reason why we should desire a reunion with the Northern Church,"[2] especially in view of actions which, according to the Synod of South Carolina, would "injure us, and even subvert the foundations of the Christian religion."[3] The Assembly of 1865, making no reference to previous statements about Church organizations following national lines, affirmed, "The reasons for its continuance not only remain as conclusive as at first, but have been exceedingly strengthened." There was a deep conviction that God had raised up the Southern Church for a special witness to the "Crown Rights of the Redeemer." Accordingly, the Macon Assembly made plans for the future and adopted a new name, "The Presbyterian Church in the United States."

The Assembly addressed a pastoral letter to its churches. The members were exhorted to "obey them that have the rule over you," and "fulfil with scrupulous fidelity all your obligations to the governments of the land." They were reminded of their duty to the Negroes. "Debtors before to them when bound, you are still debtors to them free." And the Presbyterians were challenged with the magnitude of the task before them. Though poor and afflicted, "you will educate your ministry, and then amply support them . . . You will supply your people with the printed truth in every proper form of it . . . You will plant churches where they are needed; you will push church enterprise into every accessible part of the land. The Holy Spirit will be poured out from on high. Our desolation shall be repaired, until 'streams shall break out in the desert, and the wilderness shall blossom as the rose.' "[4]

MEETING THE DESPERATE NEED
OF THE CHURCHES

The most pressing problem was the condition of the churches at home. Ministers were destitute, some of the ablest becoming schoolteachers to secure sufficient income to feed their families. A great number of congregations were without any provision for services of worship. Many sanctuaries had been destroyed, and others were in near ruin. These conditions had to be faced during the tyranny and confusion of Reconstruction, and during years when there were also famine and depression.

The task was the responsibility of the Committee of Domestic Missions, led by Dr. J. Leighton Wilson. Synodical Commissioners were appointed to survey the field to determine the needs "of every destitute brother." Two hundred and twenty ministers or their families were aided "from $50 and under, to $300." The Church did all of this, and more. Funds were provided for relief of widows and orphans of pastors, and a small pension plan was begun to provide for the future retirement of ministers still active. Aid of "from $100 to $1,000" was extended to repair or rebuild churches, but only "where the people themselves had gone to work . . ." Recognizing that the great task for the present "is not so much to establish new churches, as to keep life and energy in those already established,"[5] the Church began raising a Sustentation Fund, and in 1866 changed the name of the Committee of Domestic Missions to the Committee of Sustentation. Amid the trials of these years the Presbyterians affirmed: "The Church of God remains, and her preachers and people arise and quit themselves like men."[6]

TWO NEW SYNODS JOIN THE SOUTHERN CHURCH

The Church was aided in this work by the generosity of friends of other sections. The Board of Aid for Southern Presbyterian Pastors was an expression of the concern of friends in Kentucky. Contributions also came from Maryland and later from the Southern Aid Society of New York. The ability of the Church to meet the task was also increased by strength that came through mergers. When negotiations with the Associate Reformed Church were terminated in 1866, the Alabama Presbytery of that group sought admission to the Southern Church and was received by the Synod of Alabama. The Associate Reformed Presbytery of Kentucky was received in 1869. To both of these presbyteries it was granted that "in their worship and in the ministration of the gospel, they shall be undisturbed in their usages"[7]—that meant they could still use "their time-honored Psalmody." In 1867 the new Presbytery of Patapsco in Maryland, formed by a small group dissatisfied with the "political" deliverances of the Northern Church, was received into the Synod of Virginia. The largest unions were those with the Synod of Kentucky and the Synod of Missouri.

In 1869 commissioners from seven presbyteries in Kentucky were enrolled in the Southern Assembly. They represented almost 10,000 members, about three fourths of all the Presbyterians in that state. The division there was in part due to differences in theology and church government. But there were other factors. Kentucky was a border state; some of its citizens favored the South and some favored the North. The Presbyterians had the additional difficulty of having two outstanding leaders who were in a bitter fight with each other. Dr. Robert J. Breckinridge—in church courts he seemed "always either speaking, or just about to speak, or just through speaking"[8]—led the Presbyterians of Northern sympathies. His opponent, Dr. Stuart Robinson, sometimes showing a contentious spirit, led the pro-Southern forces. Breckinridge's *Danville Review* and Robinson's *True Presbyterian* gave each access to the printed page for hurling epithets. Without this bitter conflict the Presbyterians of Kentucky might have been able to work out their differences.

Both Breckinridge and Robinson, with a majority of the Kentucky Presbyterians, had condemned the Gardiner Spring Resolutions of 1861. They also agreed to remain in the Northern Church in spite of that deliverance. After this their paths divided. Breckinridge was influential in leading the Northern Church to stronger deliverances on the affairs of the country. Robinson, and an increasing number of members in the Synod, objected to the whole trend in the Northern Church, including the strong condemnations of slavery of the 1864 Assembly and the 1865 actions directed at the Southern Church. Northern missionaries were encouraged to reclaim the Southern territory. Any Southern minister or member who sought admission into the Northern Church would have to prove his loyalty to the United States government, his acceptance of the deliverances on slavery, and give evidence of repentance for any aid given to the "Rebellion."

All of this, said Robinson, is none of the Church's business. Dr. Robinson had spent much of his early ministry in Virginia. His Southern sympathies were obvious. In addition, he held Dr. Thornwell's interpretation of the spiritual function of the Church. His own view was shared by a majority in his Louisville Presbytery. They led the way in drawing up in 1865 a "Declaration and Testimony." This was a protest against the Northern Church's departure from the "faith and practice enjoined by her King and Head" and the "true spiritual and divine nature of her calling and work," and against the alliance "which has been virtually formed with the State."

The severity of the Northern Church against the signers of the Declaration and Testimony is explained in part by the fact that it was more than a protest. It was defiance. The signers refused to support any officers of the Church who accepted the preceding "heresies." They would not sustain or execute the actions of the Assembly on slavery or loyalty. They refused to contribute to any of the Church boards (except Foreign Missions) or seminaries. They called for a convention of all in the Church who shared their views, looking to the formation of another Church made up of conservative men. The paper was so strong that the Synod of Kentucky, with a majority dissatisfied with the Assembly actions, opposed it for "looking to the further agitation of the Church, if not its division."[9] This Declaration and Testimony was condemned by the 1866 Assembly. Its signers were summoned to the 1867 Assembly and were denied a seat in any church court higher than a session until their case was decided. Any court receiving one of the signers as a member was "ipso facto dissolved." The Assembly had the blessing of Dr. Breckinridge in these actions.

In the meeting of the Synod of Kentucky in the fall of 1866 an effort was made to apply the Assembly rulings. Over this issue the synod divided. Three fourths of the churches and members adhered to Dr. Robinson's "Southern synod." It was this group that was welcomed by the Southern Presbyterians. The Kentucky division resulted in the famous Walnut Street Church decision on church property. The Supreme Court decided in favor of the part of the congregation allied with Dr. Breckinridge's synod because, though much smaller, that synod was recognized by the Assembly as the true body. ". . . the courts of law must accept as final and conclusive the decision of the General Assembly on subjects purely ecclesiastical."[10] This principle was welcomed by the Northern Church. It was condemned by the Southern Presbyterians—but often approved and used since!—on the ground that no accidental majority in a General Assembly should determine property rights, and because it was not the principle followed in the 1837 division.

Troubles in Missouri were similar to those in Kentucky. That, too, was a border synod and experienced the division of sympathies. There were many signers of the Declaration and Testimony.

A division resulted in two synods. Affirming "the great principle —exclusiveness of the spiritual vocation of the church,"[11] the larger synod, with six presbyteries, sixty-seven ministers, and about 8,000 members, came into the Southern Church.

One of the heroic characters who became a Southern Presbyterian was Dr. S. B. McPheeters of St. Louis. Though he had twice taken an oath of allegiance to the Federal government, when war came he determined on a policy of silence and neutrality and an avoidance of all political preaching and praying. By this approach he hoped to avoid division in his congregation composed of Northern and Southern people. The military authorities, " on the basis of unmistakable evidence" that he was sympathetic with the "Rebellion," forbade him to discharge his ministerial functions and ordered him to leave the state. Dr. McPheeters took the case to Washington. Lincoln responded with his famous letter, ". . . the United States government must not . . . undertake to run the Churches."[12] When the military authorities ordered church courts to determine whether each member had taken the oath of allegiance within a specified time, Dr. McPheeters and others absented themselves from Presbytery rather than become involved in this mixture of Church and State. The remaining small minority of Presbytery dissolved the pastoral relation between Dr. McPheeters and the Pine Street (now Westminster) Church. Dr. McPheeters appealed to the General Assembly, but, in the excitement of the war years when the Northern Church sought to give every evidence of patriotism, he was not sustained. During his last years he served the old Mulberry Church near Shelbyville, Kentucky.

ADVANCE ON ALL FRONTS

The Southern Church, by 1870, had accomplished much of the work of sustaining and strengthening the feeble churches. Energies were now devoted more and more to evangelistic endeavor, much of it west of the Mississippi. By the end of Reconstruction in 1877 an aggressive home mission program had been developed.

In some states gains in church membership were of greater proportion than the increase in population. New churches were organized. Returning prosperity made possible the erection of new buildings. Synodical Home Missions were begun. In 1879 the name of the Assembly's committee was changed from Sustentation to Home Missions. This was followed in 1882 with the election of an Executive Secretary of Home Missions, and thus relief was granted to Dr. J. Leighton Wilson, who had served as Executive Secretary for Home and Foreign Missions for almost twenty years. In 1886 the headquarters of Home Missions were moved to Atlanta.

This committee had also under its oversight the evangelization of the Negroes. After the war the majority of Negroes was no longer willing to remain as a part of white congregations, with seats in the galleries or at separate services. Many of the white people also were unhappy with this arrangement now that the slaves were free, because it might lead to "social intermingling." Thus large independent Negro denominations were formed. Negroes left the Southern Presbyterian Church in great numbers. Some Negro churches were given financial aid by the Board of National Missions of the Northern Church and became a part of that body. The Southern Assembly of 1865 expressed the hope that Negroes and white people might continue "united together in the worship of God," but admitted that the Negroes were no longer "crowding the courts of the Lord," and that "comparatively but few of them are seen in the assemblies of the saints."[13]

Various experiments were tried by the Church. The Assembly of 1866 approved branch congregations under white sessions, and authorized the licensing of qualified Negroes as exhorters. This action was unsatisfactory to the Synod of Virginia and the Presbytery of Mississippi. They sent up overtures calling on the Assembly to authorize presbyteries "to ordain to the gospel ministry, and to organize into separate congregations, duly qualified persons of the colored race, and so declare that mere race or color is not regarded as a bar to office or privilege in the Presbyterian Church in the United States."[14] The 1867 Assembly replied that the presbyteries had the sole responsibility of judging the qualifications and of ordaining men "of whatever race, color, or civil condition," according to the rules of the Church and "in the exercise of a sound Christian discretion." It was not until 1874 that the Church moved from the plan of branch or separate congregations under white sessions, or under Negro sessions whose elders could not be members of presbytery.

In that year the Assembly, availing itself of "the additional light which experience has thrown upon this important question,"[15] began promoting the formation of fully organized Negro churches under Negro ministers and sessions. These were, in time, to be formed into separate presbyteries and synods and finally into a separate, independent General Assembly. The year 1874 saw also the establishment of the Colored Evangelistic Fund. Plans were laid for the training of Negro ministers, and in 1877 the Church, led by Dr. C. A. Stillman, opened an institution, now Stillman College, at Tuscaloosa, Alabama.

In the meantime the work of Foreign Missions was not neglected. "We can scarcely set up a claim to be regarded as a true branch of the Church of Christ, or take an honorable place in the sisterhood of evangelical churches," said Dr. J. Leighton Wilson to the Assembly in 1865, "unless we keep this object constantly and distinctly before our minds."[16] In addition to the continuing Indian work, a mission in China was authorized in 1866, and the first missionary sailed in 1867. In that year work was also begun in Italy, in Colombia and Brazil in 1869, in Mexico and Greece in 1874, and in Japan in 1885. Work in each area was small, the force consisting in many cases of one missionary or a couple. In some instances the Church simply assumed the support of missionaries who had been in the field previously. But the responsibility had been acknowledged; growth would follow in later years. In days of financial hardship, when the Committee of Foreign Missions was in debt and the cry was for retrenchment and reform for all agencies, the Assembly "bid the Committee go forward wisely, prudently, courageously, hopefully, trustfully, in the glorious work committed to its hand."

The Missionary, begun in 1867, was the medium of keeping the Church informed about the work. A manual for missionaries and candidates was approved in 1877. The discussion of the relations of the missionary to the "native church" led to the policy, in the interest of developing national Churches, that ordinarily missionaries should not become "associated with natives in the composition of presbyteries." This policy, in which the Southern Church pioneered, has continued to be basic in its missionary approach, though departed from for a period. The resignation of Dr. Wilson, after almost twenty-five years as Executive Secretary, marked the end of an era which appeared symbolized by the movement of the office to Nashville in 1889.

Growth in missionary outreach was accompanied by educational expansion. There was an increase in the number of the Church's colleges. King College was opened in 1867, Arkansas College in 1872, Southwestern, though having elements of earlier origin, in 1875 as an outgrowth of the movement for a great Southern Presbyterian university, and Presbyterian College in South Carolina in 1880. The founding of Thornwell Orphanage by William Plumer Jacobs in 1875 was a symbol of the work of the Church in this area.

Among the seminaries, Union recovered from the disasters of the war through the work of Dr. B. M. Smith. Columbia Seminary emerged from its destitution only to pass through a time of trial which lasted throughout this period. Danville Seminary was awarded to the Northern Church after the division in Kentucky and was to have no Southern Church connection for three decades. The foundations of a fourth seminary were laid at this time. In 1883 Dr. Robert L. Dabney, the professor of theology at Union Seminary, went to the University of Texas as professor of moral and mental philosophy. He and Dr. R. K. Smoot, pastor of the First Southern Presbyterian Church in Austin, founded in 1884 the Austin School of Theology, under the control of Central Texas Presbytery. On this foundation was later built Austin Presbyterian Seminary to meet the needs of the growing Southwest. There was begun the Divinity School of Southwestern Presbyterian University in Clarksville, Tennessee, but it was discontinued after about thirty years. Theological education received much attention in the Assemblies of this period as the Church sought to define its responsibility for ministerial candidates and to determine the best course of training.

Determination of policies and principles in all areas was a principal concern. The Revision of the Form of Government and Book of Discipline was completed in 1879. Changes in the constitution inherited from the Northern Church had been under consideration for eighteen years and were in the direction of decentralization. The ruling elder was considered essential for a quorum of presbytery and was to "lay on hands" in the ordination of a minister. The layman's right to be moderator of a church court or to preach the moderatorial sermon was not clearly granted for some years. Deacons were given increased status and work. The authority of deliverances of General Assemblies produced a memorable debate in the Assembly of 1880 but the issue was soon settled. Dwight L. Moody's success in revivals led to enthusiasm for "lay-evangelism," but this did not find ready acceptance in the Church. While the opportunities of elders in neighboring churches were given emphasis, the preaching of the Word was recognized as belonging to the ordained ministry. In worship, several attempts were made to secure "a few Scriptural and well considered forms of prayer, requiring responses on the part of the congregation," but they met overwhelming defeat. The Directory of Worship was revised, and several hymnbooks were given approval through the years. Opposition to instrumental music in the churches still had the support of a few prominent ministers, but to no avail.

No subject received more attention than the spiritual nature and function of the Church. There was constant restatement or reaffirmation of this theme. A pamphlet on the "Distinctive Principles" of the Church was a collection of the Southern Presbyterian pronouncements on this subject. Committees were appointed to search the Assembly records "to the end that no vestige of anything inconsistent with the clearly defined position of our

General Assemblies may be left to impair the testimony of our Church upon this vital point."[17] This testimony by word and life to the spirituality of the Church, it was believed, was the reason why, in the providence of God, the Southern Church had been raised up.

END OF ISOLATION: JOINING THE WORLD PRESBYTERIAN ALLIANCE

A significant change in the life of the Church took place during these years. There had been expressed the desire to cultivate fellowship with all Christians; fraternal relations had been established with other Presbyterian bodies in the South, and negotiations with the Reformed Church in America had taken place. But Southern Presbyterians were living very much apart. This was acceptable to many. "Let us in our feebleness, in our isolation . . . work out our destiny until the Lord pushes us to the front to do the great work in propagating our principles to the end of the earth," said Dr. Palmer. "Let us, in our isolation, in our obscurity, upon this plane, work out our mission. . . ."[18] Gradually the Church modified this position. Evidence of the change was given in relation to the Alliance of Reformed Churches (Presbyterian World Alliance). An invitation to join in founding that body came to the 1874 Assembly and was declined. The dissatisfaction of the Church was reflected in the 1875 Assembly which took a more positive step and authorized a delegate at the organizational meeting. The 1876 Assembly approved membership.

The opposition to the Alliance centered in New Orleans and South Carolina. Dr. H. M. Smith led the opposition in 1874, Dr. Palmer in 1875, and Dr. R. Q. Mallard in 1876. All of these were from the Presbytery of New Orleans. Dr. John B. Adger of South Carolina proved a determined opponent in the 1876 Assembly. Dr. Robert L. Dabney of Virginia gave strong support to this opposition through articles in the Presbyterian press. The arguments were varied. The Alliance was not a part of the Church "in her organized form" but an "irresponsible and voluntary association." It might grow into an "ecumenical council." Membership would mean compromise of the Southern view of slavery, not elsewhere accepted, as well as compromise with the "broad-churchism" in theology which was said to characterize the other bodies. The argument designed to carry the greatest force and win the most votes: the Southern Church would be a fellow member with the Northern Church!

Victory for entering the Alliance was due chiefly to two men. The first was Dr. Stuart Robinson of Kentucky. Since he had been a part of the most conservative wing in the Church, his stand indicated that the conservatives were divided. His border state connections, as well as a brief ministry in Canada, led him away from the isolationist position. Accepting what appeared to be the position of the opposition, that the Southern Church was the only true Church, he arrived at a different conclusion. "I am not afraid to risk the Southern Presbyterian Church in any common concern in the world. Let us only have a fair and equal voice, and I am not afraid of our being overrun. I maintain that, in proportion to our numbers, though it may seem a little boastful, we have more brains and more orthodoxy than any, and can better defend ourselves in any common scrimmage. . . . Dr. Palmer suggests that we put it off till next year. My complaint is that we have been playing Rip Van Winkle long enough. This thing has been going on for two or three years, and we are going to wait until it is all fixed, and then ask for admission. Sir, I want to be at the first. I want to go in there before the door is shut and I have to be voted in by these brethren at the North. Dr. Palmer speaks of his pride in the glorious truths which we hold, and in being isolated in the teaching of them. Sir, I trust I love those truths, and I have as much admiration of them, and I feel as proud, as he, when I hear even the Northern brethren speak of us, as I have heard them, as the purest body of Presbyterians in the world; but I think Dr. Palmer mistakes his calling in what he says about holding them in isolation. That is not my notion. If we have got a pure Presbyterianism, I want to go and tell it to somebody else. I want 'to tell to sinners round,' what a glorious gospel we have found. It is not our business to 'hide our light under a bushel.' Jesus Christ told us to preach the gospel to every creature. I want to get our Presbyterianism into the 'frontier and destitute settlements' of the North. . . . As I told the Nashville Assembly, the grand trouble with the Southern Church was, that in the command to 'go, teach all nations,' they interpreted the 'all nations' to mean their side of the Potomac and Ohio. I do not believe in that. We have got the true thing; we have the true metal, and I want to go out and ring it in the ear of these Moderates, and No-Churchmen, and broad-Churchmen. I want to put ourselves in the position where our testimony for Jesus Christ, and for a pure Church, will be heard—not to stand here in our isolation and the world know nothing about it."[19]

The great leader in the victory for the Alliance was Dr. Moses Drury Hoge of Richmond, Virginia. Contacts at home and abroad had increased his appreciation of other Presbyterian bodies. His remarks in the 1876 Assembly were not based on the premise of Dr. Robinson. ". . . have we not a guarantee in the character of the great churches which are represented in the Alliance that they will not betray the interests which are as dear to them as to ourselves? Have they nothing at stake? Have not the men who made Christ's crown and covenant their watchword regard for the honor of the Redeemer and the purity of the church? Are they the men to dishonor their own traditions and to violate the constitutions of their own churches? If we cannot trust them, whom can we trust? . . . Who are the men who cannot bear the test of the light of our purity? Is there no genuine Presbyterianism but ours? If the only pure Church is the Presbyterian Church of these Southern States; if the problem of the development of Christianity as symbolized in the Presbyterian faith and form of government has been solved only by us; if after all the great sacrifices of confessors and martyrs of past ages, we alone constitute the true Church; if this only is the result of the stupendous sacrifice on Calvary, and the struggles of apostles and missionaries and reformers in all generations; then may God have mercy on the world and on His Church. Moderator, when night casts its mantle over the earth, and one by one the constellations of heaven shine forth until the whole sky is illumined with their glory, how would it look for one star on the southern horizon to say, 'I am the heavenly host?' When a fleet is drawn up for a naval engagement, and monitors, and seventy-fours, and iron-clads are ranged for action, how would it look for a single gunboat to proclaim, 'I am the fleet?' . . . Let us not be suspicious of other Churches of like faith and order with ourselves, but, taking the word and relying on the honor of God's ministers and office-bearers in the eldership, let us see if we cannot help them by our coöperation, and be helped by them, as we plan and labor together in the unity of the Spirit and in the bonds of peace."[20]

FRATERNAL RELATIONS WITH THE PRESBYTERIAN CHURCH IN THE U.S.A.

The real test of the movement away from Dr. Palmer's isolation came with respect to establishing fraternal relations, through official exchange of delegates, with the Northern Church. For a time Northern Presbyterians hoped that with the end of the war the two Churches would be reunited. Dr. Charles Hodge and other conservatives labored to maintain in the Northern Church a spirit and a conduct that would make this possible. They opposed the movement for union with the New School Church lest this hinder reunion with the Southern Church. The Northern Church retained the Southern presbyteries and synods on its roll until 1868. But when it became clear that the Southern Church was not "hanging about the church door and asking for admittance," the independent existence of the Southern Church was acknowledged. The Northern Assembly in 1869 expressed the desire "that the day may not be distant when we may again be united in one great organization." Their merger with the New School Church took place in 1870. Realizing that this postponed the day of union with the Southern Church, the united Northern Church sent to the Southern Assembly of 1870 a message and three delegates to express the desire "for the speedy establishment of cordial, fraternal relations . . . upon terms of mutual confidence, respect, Christian honor, and love . . ."[21]

Establishing even fraternal relations through exchange of official delegates was no simple matter for the Southern Presbyterians. They feared that this first step would lead logically and inevitably to union, and they in no way found this an acceptable possibility. Even fraternal relations were hard. The wounds of the war were deep and not yet healed. Had not the Northern Church virtually expelled them in 1861? Had it not continued its political deliverances and actions? Did not the records of that Church contain many references to the "rebellion" and "treason" of the South and to the "schism" and heretical and blasphemous opinions on slavery of the Southern Church? Had not the Northern Presbyterians declared after the war that they would give special attention to the Southern field, as if with the purpose of sowing division in the churches? Had they not established a new test of "orthodoxy" for any Southern ministers or members seeking admission into the Northern Church, that these must prove their loyalty, their repudiation of the Southern view of slavery, and their repentance for any acts of rebellion? Further, could the Southern Church have official fraternal relations with a group that so recently had cut off those Presbyterians in Kentucky who were now fellow members in the Southern Church? And was not the reunion with the New School a sacrifice of doctrinal soundness? All of this Dr. Palmer reviewed, in preparation for the 1870 Assembly, through seventeen articles in the *Southwestern Presbyterian* in the fall of 1869. The material was published in pamphlet form, and twenty-five hundred copies were distributed.

When the Southern Assembly opened in Louisville in 1870, all was in readiness. Dr. Robert L. Dabney had been charged in advance to see that a "shrewd committee" was appointed to handle the proposals expected from the Northern Presbyterians. He was in good position to do this when he was elected Moderator. He named Dr. Palmer as chairman of the Committee on Foreign Correspondence.

Soon the Northern delegation arrived, disavowing any plans

for union but asking that the Southern Church appoint a committee to confer with a similar committee to be appointed by the Northern Church on establishing fraternal relations. The delegation was composed of three men who were "so particularly acceptable to us,"[22] said Dr. Stuart Robinson. The chairman was Dr. Henry J. Van Dyke. He was conservative, long a friend of the South, moderate in his view of slavery, an opponent of the political deliverances of the Church, and a signer of the Declaration and Testimony. All of the delegates made a favorable impression. When the Assembly met at night as a Committee of the Whole, there appeared a disposition to accept their proposals. But Dr. Dabney, not then presiding, rose to speak. "Mr. Chairman . . . I hear brethren saying it is time to forgive. Mr. Chairman, I do not forgive. I do not try to forgive. What! forgive these people, who have invaded our country, burned our cities, destroyed our homes, slain our young men, and spread desolation and ruin over our land! No, I do not forgive them."[23] The tide was turned! While the Assembly agreed to appoint a committee, it laid down as "four indispensable conditions," removal of difficulties with respect to political deliverances, union with the New School, treatment of Presbyterians in Kentucky, and accusations against the Southern Church. The conditions were in reality, said a protest in the Southern Assembly minutes, charges against the Northern Church, and, according to another protest, represented an attitude "discourteous," "offensive," "palpably, and to many of us painfully, variant from the placable and charitable spirit of the gospel of peace and good will."[24] A pastoral letter was sent to Southern Presbyterians explaining the Assembly's decision and the hindrances in the way of fraternal relations. It was drawn up by Dr. Palmer and approved by the Assembly.

Dr. Van Dyke said, "They have stripped every leaf from the olive branch, and made a rod of it to beat us with."[25] The Northern Church discharged its committee and postponed action. The Southern position, it was stated, involved "a virtual prejudgement of the very difficulties concerning which we invited the conference." Presbyterian papers in the South gave the Northern Church credit for breaking off negotiations.

In 1874 the subject was renewed. The Northern Assembly sent another invitation to hold a conference. This time the Southern Church appointed a committee, with Dr. Palmer as a member, "without any official instructions." The two committees met in the same building in Baltimore but carried on negotiations in writing. They discussed accusations and disagreements about property rights.

Most of the meeting was devoted to "unjust and injurious accusations" made against the Southern Church. "If you [your Assembly] could see your way clear," said the Southern Committee, "to say in a few plain words to this effect, that these obnoxious things were said in times of great excitement, that they are to be regretted, and that now, in a calm review, the imputations cast upon the Southern Church disapproved, that could end the difficulty at once."[26] The Northern reply was: "We cannot make this recommendation to our Assembly, for the reason that its actions for the last four years, so fully recited to you in our last communication, constitute a sufficient ground for fraternal correspondence." On this note the meeting came to a close.

Southern Presbyterians were looking for "one manly expression of regret for the injurious imputations heaped on us for so many years." It appeared to them that the Northern Assembly could easily take such action but would not. At this distance of several decades it appears that a simple straightforward apology was not made. But it may not have appeared so to the Northern Presbyterians. They had declared that any accusation against the Southern Church "has been since the reunion, and is now, null and void," and expressed in their Assembly records their confidence in the soundness of doctrine and Christian character of the Southern Church. Dr. Van Dyke was a member of the Northern Committee at Baltimore. He had only two years previous to the Baltimore Conference served for a brief time as pastor of the First Presbyterian Church of Nashville. His views were acceptable to this portion of the South, and he was considered trustworthy by Presbyterians there. He supported the unanimous position of the Northern Committee at Baltimore. The Southern Church with its continuing affirmation, "Having placed nothing in the way of Christian fraternity, there was nothing for us to remove,"[27] may have been a difficult group with which to deal.

The attitude of the Southern Church began to change gradually. Dr. Palmer wrote in 1876 that he was not hopeful of the future. Dr. Dabney was called "wrangler" and "old war horse." In 1876 the Assembly said, "Misapprehension exists in the minds of some of our people" about the Southern Church's attitude at Baltimore. There developed in succeeding years in both Churches a disposition against impugning the Christian character of the other body. In 1882 four overtures came up to the Southern Assembly calling for closer relations. By a large vote the Southern Assembly, departing from "the quiet expectation of approach from the other side," seized the initiative and sent a telegram to the Northern Assembly, "While receding from no principle, we do hereby declare our regret for and withdrawal of all expressions of our Assembly which may be regarded as reflecting upon, or offensive to, the General Assembly of the Presbyterian Church in the United States of America."[28] The Northern Assembly returned the exact expression with regard to the Southern Church. A second telegram signed by the Northern Moderator stated that the regret and withdrawal applied only to accusations of schism and heresy, not to expressions about the loyalty and rebellion of the South. This caused pain and indignation but did not deter the Southern Church. Fraternal relations were approved, and in 1883 there was an exchange of official delegates.

TWENTY-FIFTH BIRTHDAY

In 1886 the Assembly met again in the First Presbyterian Church, under "the ancient oaks," in Augusta, Georgia, to observe its Quarter-Centennial. There were three addresses, each made by a minister who had been a member of the first Assembly twenty-five years before. Dr. Joseph R. Wilson, pastor of the Augusta Church in 1861 and father of Woodrow Wilson, gave the memorial address. The address on Christian education was delivered by Dr. John N. Waddell. The principal address was by

Dr. Palmer, on the subject "The Church a Spiritual Kingdom." "The historic basis, therefore, upon which stands this dear Church of ours, the special feature by which she is distinguished from others, is this testimony for Christ's Kingdom, as a free, spiritual Commonwealth . . . It is no unimportant mission to which we have been assigned in the adorable providence of God —not lightly entered upon in 1861, not lightly to be abandoned in the future. May grace be given us 'to preach this Gospel of the Kingdom,' until the captive bride of Christ shall exchange her 'fetters of brass' for 'clothing wrought of gold'; when 'the light of the moon shall be upon her as the light of the sun, and the light of the sun shall be sevenfold, as the light of seven days, in the day that the Lord bindeth up the breach of the people, and healeth the stroke of their wound.' "[29]

The Church in the New South

"THE NEW SOUTH"! This was one of those popular slogans that became a rallying cry. Not all of the South was new by any means. Many of the old problems remained, some of them grown worse. But there was a new state of mind or attempt to promote a new state of mind. War and Reconstruction were considered as past; what was important now was the future. There existed a new optimism and idealism, a new unity, and increased determination. Soon there were evidences of improvement.

By the early 1880's signs of economic recovery appeared, though not for twenty years was there regained the measure of prosperity enjoyed in 1860. With new leadership and capital, emphasis was placed on industrial development. Textile mills, paper industries, lumber yards, and iron and steel plants were multiplied. The South's petroleum industry was born. Railroads and shipping were greatly increased. Cotton, rice, and tobacco crops were expanded. The General Assembly of 1883 was told that towns were springing up, that mining, manufacturing, and commercial centers were being formed, and that large areas of the country were being filled up with an enterprising population. There were also gains in other areas. A literary awakening took place in the 1880's and, after a period of barrenness, flourished again in the 1920's. Recovery, though slow, was made in scholarship and higher learning. A rapid growth in membership increased the influence of the Churches. The New South was on the way! The whole area presented an inviting and promising field for the aggressive work of God's people.

CONTROVERSY OVER EVOLUTION

One of the aims of the "New South" movement was to overcome isolation, to be again a part of the nation, not just a region. One of the results was that there flowed into the Southern states, as elsewhere, strange new currents. Charles Darwin had written *Origin of Species*. Wellhausen and other Biblical scholars had done intensive study on the authorship and unity of the books of the Bible. When evolution and Biblical criticism were brought to America there followed controversy in the Churches over the new ideas. In some denominations long, bitterly fought heresy trials took place. For the Southern Presbyterians evolution was the disturbing factor. Not many in the Church knew what evolution meant, and fewer still accepted it. But it produced the greatest controversy the Church had known up to that time—or since! It was the major issue before the Church from 1884 to 1888, and continued a source of difficulty until 1894.

The central figure was a brilliant and, in many ways, lovable man, Dr. James Woodrow, uncle of Woodrow Wilson. Woodrow became in 1861 the first Perkins professor of natural science at Columbia Seminary. The establishment of this professorship, designed "to evince the harmony of science with the records of our faith and to refute the objections of Infidel Naturalists,"[1] was a notable and pioneering step. For twenty years Dr. Woodrow satisfactorily filled the post, until in 1882 rumors about his views were increasingly repeated. To set everything straight the professor gave a full and frank review of his position in 1884, admitting that whereas formerly he opposed the hypothesis of the evolution of Adam's body, he now believed it to be probably true. Adam's body (but not Eve's), he said, probably evolved like that of a horse!

The controversy was on! Before it was over Columbia Seminary lost three of its four professors (including Woodrow), experienced a change of fifty per cent in its Board of Directors, and was closed for a year. Eight Presbyterian weeklies in the South were filled with charges and countercharges and with long scientific articles and editorials. One hundred and four ministers signed a "Declaration and Testimony" which appeared to point in the direction of division. Two Assemblies condemned evolution, and the action was protested as a violation of the spiritual mission of the Church.

Dr. Woodrow put up a terrific fight and had many supporters. Not many shared his views but they contended for his liberty to hold them and against condemnation of him without a trial. Dr. Woodrow had several interests in the contest. He defended his honor against the accusation that he was "another Socrates— corrupting the minds of the youth of our ecclesiastical Athens,"[2] and that he held views in violation of his oath as a minister and professor. He fought for "untrammeled freedom of inquiry," and to refute the idea that the Southern Church was afraid of honest and independent investigation. He battled for youth and scientists, lest they be driven from the Church by the idea that science and the Bible conflict. And he contended for the spiritual mission of the Church, holding that as the Church had no business making political deliverances, it had no right to make scientific declarations. "Oh, Moderator," he said, "it will be a sad day when this Synod resolves itself into an association for determining the exact amount of truth in a purely scientific proposition."[3]

Dr. Woodrow also had an abundance of opponents. His "hand of iron under a glove of silk" did not endear him to all. In the evolution controversy his chief opponent was Dr. John L. Girardeau, a colleague on the Columbia faculty. These two met in a tremendous debate at the 1884 meeting of the Synod of South Carolina. Woodrow's speech lasted for five hours (fatigue forced him to stop; he concluded the speech the next day!) and Girardeau's only slightly less. The two met again in a dramatic scene before the Synod of Georgia, when Girardeau, witness for the prosecution, was cross-examined by Woodrow. Girardeau's interest was theological. The group he represented was concerned for the bearing of evolution on the faith of the Church. For them the acceptance of the evolution of Adam's body meant that "the doctrines of the federal headship of Adam, the descent of all men from Adam, original sin, etc., must all be abandoned."[4] As the correspondent of the *New York Observer* wrote, they had no use for "tadpole theology." Woodrow could not see that the faith was imperiled. He thought it was a matter of how one interpreted "dust"—was it organic or inorganic? Since the Bible was not explicit he felt free to interpret "dust" as meaning organic matter.

After two years of controversy in Columbia's four supporting synods, the matter came to the 1886 Assembly by overture and to the 1888 Assembly on complaint of Woodrow. On neither occasion did the Assembly leave any doubt about its stand. The 1888 Assembly stated, "Now, therefore, it is the judgment of the General Assembly that Adam's body was directly fashioned by God of the dust of the ground, without any animal parentage of any kind."[5] This declaration was in effect a condemnation of Woodrow's views as contrary to Scripture and the Standards. But when Woodrow officially notified his presbytery of the action, the presbytery declared "the ecclesiastical standing of Dr. Woodrow [has] been in no respect impaired by the action . . . of the General Assembly."[6] His presbytery sent him to the 1889 Assembly and he was nominated, but not elected, to the office of Moderator of the Assembly! His standing as a minister was never questioned in presbytery, synod, or Assembly. All of this appeared to say that one could accept the views he held and remain a minister in good standing in the Church.

The controversy was a painful experience but not without some gains. The necessity of the Church's limiting its work to "the legitimate sphere of ecclesiastical action" was more deeply impressed. Encouragement was found in the vigorous battle for orderly procedures and against any condemnation without a trial provided for in the constitution of the Church, and in the strength of the opposition to anything interpreted as undermining the faith. The willingness of so many to wrestle with the meaning of the Christian faith in the light of new challenges came as a welcome surprise. Through this controversy the Church was seeking new light on pressing problems. What is the role of a denominational seminary? Is "the genius of the Theological Seminary . . . dogmatic" or is its genius "that of inquiry into all truth"?[7] Where is the theology of the Church to be found? Is it in the Bible, in the interpretation of the Bible, in the Standards, in "accepted interpretation" and "received views," or in the living voice of the Church as it declares in succeeding church courts what the Bible and the Standards mean in each situation? The Church was not weaker for having wrestled with these issues, though no official answers were given at that time.

Perhaps because of the evolution controversy the Church had no battle over Biblical criticism. With the conservatism of the Church the matter was hardly seriously discussed. In Southern Presbyterian newspapers there were brief and condescending remarks about those who thought there was more than one account of the flood and the plagues of Egypt in the book of Genesis. There was no place for two Isaiahs for Southern Presbyterians! The Church also let pass by for the time the rising "social gospel" movement. Others could talk about society; Southern Presbyterians would preach the gospel to individuals.

TRAINING LAYMEN FOR LEADERSHIP

A remarkable aspect of the evolution controversy was the prominent part played by laymen. Elders, for example, supported Woodrow in greater proportion than did ministers. One of the most significant developments in this whole period was the increasing activity of laymen, and the provision by the Church for their training and service. Men's organizations were encouraged with the aim of establishing a "Presbyterian Brotherhood" in every local church. A notable challenge to the men came through the Church's participation in the Layman's Missionary Movement. Great conventions were held, and there was an enthusiastic enlistment of men in support of the foreign mission work. The increasing activity led to the 1922 Assembly's approval of the Permanent Committee on Men's Work and efforts for an organization in every presbytery and synod.

Young people's societies, known as Westminster Leagues, began to function. The Assembly in 1893 recognized this as "the most distinctive and conspicuous feature of the life of the Church today." However, the movement was slow in developing, in part because many pastors were afraid of boys and girls meeting together and of girls taking part on programs! An agreement was reached that "when Sessions prefer to keep the sexes separate, societies for boys under sixteen years of age [may] be called 'Covenanter Companies,' and societies for girls and young women [may] be called 'Miriam Chapters' "!8 For many years the denominational program was promoted, but the tide for Christian Endeavor proved too strong, so that the Assembly in 1916 recognized this form of youth work. Beginnings were made with local councils, presbytery and synod committees, and young people's conferences. These developments were encouraged by the Assembly's Superintendent of Sabbath School and Young People's Work. Much attention was given to Sunday schools. Resistance to the use of Uniform lessons and growing preference for International Graded lessons led the Church to its own graded materials.

THE ROLE OF WOMEN IN THE CHURCH

The increasing prominence of the laity is best seen in the recognition of the place of women in the Church and their increased activity. The 1880 Assembly had been asked whether the Standards prohibited women from preaching. The answer: it is "opposed to the advancement of true piety and to the promotion of peace in the Church,"9 and therefore was not to be tolerated. Not only was preaching by women not allowed, but, said the 1891 Assembly, "public speaking in the promiscuous assembly of the congregation or church is contrary to the Holy Oracles, and, therefore, should be prohibited and condemned by the presbyteries and Sessions."10 They should hold meetings among themselves, devise ways of aiding church work, and teach in the Sabbath school!

The matter of women speaking in churches, for all the condemnation voiced, did not rest. More than one Assembly had to repeat the prohibition. Finally an Ad-Interim Committee studied the matter and led the 1916 Assembly to repeat its condemnation of preaching by women but declare that as for other services, they are "left to the discretion of the Sessions and the enlightened conscience of our Christian women themselves."[11] So the door was opened, and has remained open, except for a one-year backward step in 1925 when the Assembly reaffirmed its 1891 position. In 1920 women missionaries were allowed membership and voting privilege in the missions in foreign lands. There were further advances when in 1923 the Assembly's executive committees were instructed to add three women to their membership, and when in 1926 the Assembly recognized the right of the superintendent (secretary) of the Woman's Auxiliary to read her report to the Assembly.

In the meantime an organization to promote the services of women in the Church had been established. This development was not surprising in view of the fact that in the nation a campaign for women's rights was vigorously pushed in the first decades of the twentieth century. The great advances in women's work in other denominations provided incentive for the Southern Presbyterian women. Among Southern Presbyterians, women's societies had been active in local churches for a century. Often there were several societies devoted to particular causes. It was not uncommon for a church to have a Women's Foreign Mission Society, Home Missionary Society, Bible Society, Educational Society, and Ladies' Aid Society. Sometimes there were Busy Bees, Little Gleaners, Sunshine Band, etc. Often a woman participated in only one group, and between groups there was rivalry to secure as a new member every woman who came into the church. The first development of a "presbyterial" organization of women's societies came in the 1880's. Most of these early presbyterials worked only for foreign missions. By 1904 there was the first synodical organization.

The multiplying societies and presbyterial and synodical unions, as well as the vision of the possibilities in the organization of the women, resulted in a movement to secure the appointment of a woman as General Secretary of Woman's Work. The movement, led by women in Missouri, did not receive unanimous support by any means! There was fear of an independent women's board and of a woman bishop. Many a pastor preached about Miriam as a disturber of the Camp of Israel, and likened her to women who were trying to run the Church! The leaders among the women carried on an intensive educational campaign, during which they stressed "The Nots." "We are *not* asking more authority. We are *not* asking the handling of funds. We are *not* asking the creation of a new agency. We *are* asking more efficiency through better organization and closer union of our forces."[12] The success of the campaign was crowned by the approval of the 1912 Assembly.

After the first superintendent was chosen, the organization of presbyterials and synodicals was completed, while the promotion of a single women's society in local churches was carried out as rapidly as sentiment permitted. The circle plan was inaugurated and an effective training program was developed. Presbyterials were established among the Indians, Mexicans, and Negroes. The plan was taken overseas by missionaries, and women's work was inaugurated, along the Southern Presbyterian pattern, in Mexico, Brazil, and Korea. By the tenth anniversary in 1922, membership had grown from 24,000 to 89,000 and contributions from $384,000 to $1,144,000. Nothing overcame opposition so rapidly as the success of the enterprise.

The training of laymen for service in the Church was aided by two other developments. First, in point of time, was the acquisition of Montreat in western North Carolina as a conference center for the Church. Through the generosity of some and the hard work of others Montreat was secured for "the freshening up in theological studies by our ministers, the exploiting of the departments of Christian work as conducted by our executive agencies, the promotion of Sabbath School and young people's work, and the ventilation of other plans of Christian service."[13] Facilities were enlarged, making possible conferences with annual programs of inspiration and training. Montreat became a great asset as the Church sought to train its members for life and work. Here, too, was located in 1927 the Historical Foundation of the Presbyterian and Reformed Churches.

The second development was the establishment in 1914 of the

Assembly's Training School for Lay Workers. For a brief time the Assembly had operated "The Bible and Training School" for women missionaries. New demands arose for an institution designed primarily for training lay leaders. One interest in the establishment of the school originated in the request of young women for training in preparation for service in the foreign field. Another concern was the need of trained workers in all departments of church work. The Training School for Lay Workers was placed adjacent to a seminary lest it be tempted to become a seminary, and was located in Richmond because of the offers of support.

EDUCATIONAL AND LITERARY ACTIVITY

The seminaries experienced great trial and change. Small enrollments and financial trials led to consideration of the consolidation of the seminaries into one strong institution. But it was felt that needs in various areas of the Church would not be met by a single school. Union Seminary made greatest progress. In 1898 it was moved, in spite of much opposition, from Hampden-Sydney to Richmond, to secure metropolitan advantages, make possible the observation by the students of the best methods of Christian work in actual operation, and as an aid in preparing men for a work in great centers. The leader of Union Seminary during these years was Dr. Walter W. Moore. He was one of those great religious personalities who have dominated the Southern Church, and probably exercised the greatest influence in the Church during the first quarter of the twentieth century. Columbia Seminary was moved in 1927 to Atlanta (Decatur), where it could secure a sufficient measure of financial support, and where it could render the largest service to the Church. In Kentucky, Southern Presbyterians, with no theological school after Danville Seminary was awarded to the Northern Church, provided in 1891 for theological classes at their Central University in Richmond, Kentucky, and in 1893 opened Louisville Presbyterian Theological Seminary. In 1901 the Northern and Southern Presbyterians in Kentucky merged their institutions, each group supporting Centre College and the united seminary at Louisville. In the Southwest, the Austin School of Theology was closed in 1895. The heir of that institution was opened in 1902 by the Synod of Texas as Austin Presbyterian Theological Seminary. In subsequent years the Synods of Arkansas, Oklahoma, and Louisiana, to meet the needs of their area, joined in support and control of this seminary.

The colleges of the Church fared poorly in the poverty of the South. Several were closed. Others were opened, but in the beginning none had outstanding assets. Through various campaigns, such as the Twentieth Century Fund, Semi-Centennial Fund, and Presbyterian Progressive Program, and beginning the use of the Every Member Canvass, the Church sought to strengthen educational work as well as other programs. Agnes Scott, with an affiliated relation to the Church, was established in 1889. Belhaven followed in 1894, Flora Macdonald in 1896, and Davis and Elkins in 1904. Meetings for students were begun in college churches. The importance of a ministry to college students, not only on church college campuses but also at state universities, was emphasized by a few, and in 1916 the Student Work Section of the Presbyterian Educational Association was established.

Literary output of the Church during this period was small. For the most part, with the exception of biographies of former leaders, the Presbyterian pen was idle. Discussion of religious and theological topics was carried on through *The Presbyterian Quarterly* (1887-1904) and through the *Union Seminary Magazine* (later *Union Seminary Review*) throughout the period. For a time there was a host of Presbyterian weeklies, but *The Presbyterian Standard* and *The Presbyterian of the South* were leading newspapers at the end of the period. *The Christian Observer* was a great favorite among the laymen and was read by many ministers.

SERVICE AT HOME AND ABROAD

While there was much emphasis on training, it was training for service in order that the Church could carry out its mission.

The evangelizing of the unreached in the South was a primary concern. Assembly, synod, and presbytery evangelists preached the gospel and sought to arouse the Church to its evangelistic opportunity. Revivals became a common feature of the program of local churches. Much attention was given to the "frontier." The older and stronger presbyteries and synods were encouraged to prosecute the work within their bounds and to contribute to aggressive work in weaker areas. There was a great opportunity in Texas, with its tremendous growth in population. In Oklahoma, work among the Indians was continued, and a belated attempt was made to reach "neglected . . . whites who are in the vast majority."[14] Arkansas and Louisiana and a part of New Mexico were also a part of the trans-Mississippi field which received concentrated efforts in the first two decades of the twentieth century. Florida was another area of great need and opportunity where the Church, as a result of home missionary labors, experienced rapid growth.

Many new congregations were organized in these frontier areas, as well as in the older synods. A loan fund was established to aid in building churches and manses, and sustentation aid was provided until churches came to self-support. The number and need of rural churches led to the creation of a Committee on Country Church Work and the choice of a director. The Church was challenged by the needs of the nation's capital. Interest in work there became especially strong during the presidency of Woodrow Wilson, who had been a member of the Southern Church and was the son of one of its ministers. Southern Presbyterians gave generous support to building the Church of the Pilgrims in Washington, D. C.

There were special groups within reach of the Church's ministry. Evangelistic and educational missions were provided for mountain people in Kentucky, West Virginia, Virginia, Tennessee, North Carolina, Georgia, Arkansas, and Missouri. In Texas, work among the Mexicans resulted in the formation of Texas Mexican Presbytery in 1908 and the establishment of two schools. The work among the Indians, transferred from the Foreign Mission Committee to that of Home Missions, was not productive of large numerical results. Chief emphasis was given to educational work and led to the establishment of Oklahoma Presbyterian College. Immigration brought many groups of foreigners to the Church's door. The Church's ministry was extended to Bohemians, Chinese, Cubans, Czechoslovaks, Italians, French, Germans, Hungarians, and Syrians, and included several Jewish centers.

Work among the Negroes was disappointing in its results. While many Negroes left the South for the cities of the North, many remained, but the Church was unsuccessful in reaching more than a few. A part of the responsibility for the situation was due to a general indifference among Presbyterians. The Church continued its declared policy of developing a separate and independent Negro Church. Because of its conviction that this was the best course, co-operation in this area with the Northern Church was declined, as that Church did not adhere to the policy of separation. Within the boundary of the Assembly in 1892 there were only forty Negro ministers, fifty-five churches, and about thirteen hundred members. In 1896 there were five Negro presbyteries, but only two were connected with the Assembly. An independent synod was set up in 1898, and in the following year took as its name the Afro-American Presbyterian Church. The establishment of an independent Negro Church did not improve matters; results continued to be discouraging. In 1916 the Assembly reversed its policy and established as an integral part of our Church Snedecor Memorial Synod, with four presbyteries. The chief service of the Church was in educational work. Stillman Institute was enlarged. By its training, standards for the Negro ministry were raised. Colored women's conferences were conducted by the Woman's Auxiliary. Missions to Negroes were opened in Louisville, Richmond, Atlanta, and New Orleans. One encouragement that work with Negroes furnished was in the number who served the Church as missionaries in the Congo.

The coming of World War I brought responsibilities for men in uniform. Through a war-work council, efforts were promoted in camps, in "war-production communities," and through the service of more than forty chaplains. After the war the Church contributed generously to the aid of churches in France and Belgium. During the period of the war the Assembly was not guilty of "warmongering." In the 1920's the Church joined in the peace emphasis, declaring in 1929, "The historic position of our Church is that the function of the Church is purely spiritual. We believe that this principle should apply in time of war as well as in time of peace, and that, therefore, the Church should never again bless a war, or be used as an instrument in the promotion of war."[15]

The Church prosecuted its mission abroad with vigor and great success. By 1924 there were 517 missionaries serving under the Executive Committee of Foreign Missions. The proportion of missionaries to membership was greater than that in almost all of the denominations, and the size of the work was surpassed by that of only a few Churches. A great impetus for advance came through the Forward Movement, begun in 1902, which resulted in an increase in the number of missionaries and in funds to support the work.

The determination of the Church to fulfill a mission to the whole world was affirmed in 1907 in a Missionary Platform. On the basis of the division of the mission fields into areas served by the various denominations, the Assembly accepted specific responsibility for twenty-five million people abroad. To meet this opportunity 800 missionaries and a budget of one million dollars were declared necessary. The Assembly affirmed, "Every true Church of Christ is, by virtue of its organization as a church of Christ, a missionary society, each member of which is under solemn covenant to the Head of the Church to help in the fulfillment of our commission to give the gospel to every creature." "It is the duty of those who have the proper gifts and qualifications, and who are not providentially hindered personally to obey the command of the Head of the Church to 'go' on this mission."[16] This "world missionary platform" was reaffirmed in 1908, 1914, and 1916.

Another great impetus for missionary work came through participation in the Laymen's Missionary Movement. Largely from the enthusiasm generated, the Church was able to send out many new missionaries, especially after 1912. There was also participation in the Interchurch World Movement, as well as in the first great Missionary Conference at Edinburgh, Scotland, in 1910.

Between 1890 and 1900 three new fields were entered. A mission was established in Africa in 1890, in Korea in 1892, and in Cuba, just acquired by the United States in the war with Spain, in 1899. Various circumstances kept the work in Africa in the mind of the Church. Samuel N. Lapsley and William H. Sheppard established the mission in the Kasai region of the Congo Free State. Lapsley died of fever after only two years of service, and Sheppard was the first of several Negro missionaries. The need of a steamer to transport the missionaries up and down the Congo won an outpouring of funds from the children of the Church and resulted in the *Lapsley*. Disaster struck the ship, with the loss of one missionary and twenty-three Africans. Again the children responded, and a larger steamer was provided. The sympathies of the Southern Presbyterians were further stirred by accounts of suffering and death carried in *The Missionary*. There were other troubles. One of the mission stations was burned by rebellious tribesmen, and two missionaries, Sheppard and W. M. Morrison, were tried for charges they made of atrocities against the Congolese. These experiences and the recognition of the great need resulted in an outpouring of missionaries and money.

INTEREST IN CHRISTIAN UNITY

In foreign mission work, as well as in the work at home, comity agreements had been worked out with the Northern Church. The relation between the Churches received repeated attention. Relations were cordial and messages of mutual admiration were exchanged. In spite of invitations from the Northern Church and overtures from Southern presbyteries, organic union was declined by the Southern Church, though the subject was discussed in 1887-1888, 1894-1895, and 1904-1906. Obstacles to union were seen in differences in views on the spirituality of the Church, the conduct of Negro work, the sphere of women, principles of property rights, and doctrine. At times there was strong opposition in Assemblies on the refusal of union. Many did not believe that "obstacles had not to any extent been removed" and that the "cause of truth and righteousness" was promoted by separate existence. During the period 1917-1930 the Southern Church appeared willing to form a federal union involving several Presbyterian bodies, but the Northern Church considered this no closer bond than already existed through the General Council of Reformed Churches in America.

In further work for Christian unity the Church sought union with the Associate Reformed Church, but the preservation of the "historic testimony in favor of an exclusive use of an inspired Psalmody" prevented success. A plan of union with the United Presbyterian Church was drawn up but failed to secure approval by a sufficient number of Southern presbyteries. There was participation in the first great Missionary Conference in Edinburgh, Scotland, in 1910, and in the Conferences of the Life and Work Movement and the Faith and Order Movement. The Church shared in some of the early steps taken to establish the Federal Council of the Churches of Christ in America, founded to express Christian unity, encourage united service, provide mutual advice, and promote the application of the law of Christ in every relation to human life. Membership in the Council, declined in 1911, was accepted in 1912. Some of the deliverances of the Council on "political relations, international relations, labor and capital problems, wage questions and working days, women's work, race problems, the making of laws and the enforcement of the same, treaties with foreign countries, women's full political and economic equality, and similar questions"[17] led to protests from the Assemblies and to overtures that the Church withdraw. The Council emphasized in replies that no deliverance of the Council was binding on a Church unless adopted by that Church, and that in a Council of thirty-one denominations there were different views on what was the proper role of the Church.

Many of the actions of the Council appeared a violation of the Southern Presbyterian view of the spiritual mission of the Church. While opposed to such deliverances, the Church bore witness on various matters. There were strong declarations against intemperance, the liquor traffic, gambling and lotteries, mob violence and taking human life without due process of law, child labor, and "every disobedience to established law and all disregard of constituted authority."[18] National prohibition and international arbitration were approved by Assembly actions.

While many of the pressing problems in the Southern states were given no attention, the Church sought to be the Church in the New South. According to its strength, it carried on the Kingdom's work with vigor. In 1930 there were almost 458,000 Church members, 450,000 students in Sunday schools, and, in a year of depression when contributions were reduced, more than $4,000,000 was given for benevolent work. By the end of the period the Church's presence had made a difference.

CHAPTER VII

Changing Climate

A FREQUENT ADMONITION received by home missionaries in the early 1930's was, "Have faith and courage."
Less mail, in the interest of economy, was being sent by the
reduced office force at Home Mission headquarters in Atlanta.
But the letters began with an exhortation to be brave. The advice
was needed before the "Cordially yours" at the close of the letters
could be read. Salaries of home missionaries, never adequate for
all necessities and already reduced, were to be cut again, the
letters stated. By 1931 aid for a hundred and thirty of the workers
and a hundred and sixty-eight of the projects was ended. Appropriations were cut 13% in April, 1932. Payments on these appropriations were reduced 10% in October and another 15% in
December. In the following year they were cut another 15% for
February and 10% more for March.

DEPRESSION AND WAR AFFECT THE CHURCH

This "disastrous retrenchment" resulted from the "great financial embarrassment" of the depression. Income from the churches
was reduced more than 50%. Executive committees began to
accumulate heavy debts—by 1931 the Foreign Mission Committee owed $359,000. Precautions had to be taken for "safeguarding
against excessive debt of Synods and Presbyteries." Local churches
stopped in the midst of building programs and struggled with
financial obligations that were staggering under the circumstances.
These churches, unable to meet benevolence quotas, were allowed to count the value of home-grown food sent to schools and
orphanages. The Assembly debated holding biennial meetings in
the interest of economy, and reduced the travel and meal allowance of its commissioners to $2.50 per day. Many Assembly over-

tures called for reduction of unnecessary expense. Hunger was the experience of millions, and despair was widespread.

Suffering continued for several years. By 1938 the worst of the financial depression was over. Debts were reduced, and activities of the churches and agencies were increased. The Ministers' Annuity Fund, long desired and planned, was put into effect in 1939. But trials of another sort soon followed. The Church's work in the Far East was disrupted by rising Japanese nationalism. Church schools in Korea were closed over the issue of worshiping at Shinto shrines. The invasion of China by Japan brought chaos to the Church's largest mission field, and the beginning of World War II affected the work at home and abroad.

The United States became involved in the conflict in 1941. True to its pledge, the Church, though loyal, did not bless war but in penitence confessed its sins and those of the nation and the world. It sought to give comfort and guidance as its members wrestled with the difficult decisions faced by Christian conscience, and labored to prepare for the acceptance of responsibilities and opportunities at the close of hostilities. The Church raised its voice in support of liberty of conscience, the rights of conscientious objectors, and the bases of a "Just and Durable Peace." Congregations were greatly affected by wartime conditions and restrictions. Many members went off to the armed services and others to defense industries. Families were separated. Thousands of death notices were received. For those at home the ministry of comfort was extended by local pastors. For those away, the Church, through its Defense Service Council, provided three hundred chaplains for the armed forces and extended its ministry to war industry communities and camp areas. Aid was given for war victims and refugees abroad and for "orphaned missions" cut off from support in European nations overcome by invasion.

THE CHURCH EXPERIENCES
AWAKENING AND CHANGE

During the war years the Church raised the "Home Mission

Emergency Fund" to make possible the greatest home mission advance in the history of the Southern Presbyterian Church. And following the war the Program of Progress was an expression of the determination to go forward. These actions were symbols of a new vitality in the Church that developed after the depression and especially after the war. This vitality affected every phase of the Church's life. A great awakening took place. Interest in evangelism became a keynote of Assemblies, and a new determination to reach the masses was born. "Restudy" characterized the period—as the Church rethought its role and mission.

Some changes were made in the Confession of Faith, including the addition of a chapter on the Holy Spirit, and another, "Of the Gospel," which emphasized the love of God for all men and the duty and privilege of everyone to accept the gospel. A revision of the Book of Church Order, Rules of Discipline, and Directory of Worship was undertaken. Theological currents in this country and abroad had their influence in the Southern Church in the beginnings of a dynamic Calvinism attempting to rethink the Reformation heritage. This interest in the Reformed heritage influenced a number of ministers in the use of a more formal worship.

Biblical theology, with emphasis on the message rather than the mere content of the books of the Bible, became a leading interest of the younger ministers. There was more theological preaching and greater effort to apply the gospel to life. Study was devoted to the matter of divorce and remarriage, in an attempt to ensure that the requirements of the Church expressed the spirit of the gospel, and to working out a Christian position on "faith healing." New vigor developed in intellectual life. The Presbyterian pen became active, resulting in some contributions recognized as works of sound scholarship. Through its own press the Church published books in greater number and of greater worth.

The organizational life of the Church was affected. In 1949 Assembly agencies were reconstituted to achieve "greater economy, foresight and effectiveness," and to "simplify, unify, co-ordinate and generally make more effective the total work of the General Assembly."[1] The result was five major boards—Annuities and Relief, Christian Education, Church Extension, World Missions, Women's Work. The change from executive committees to boards preserved the principle of agencies directly responsible to the Assembly. The boards, with enlarged staffs, added various departments in response to the need and demand for more services. The General Council received responsibility for co-ordinating, integrating, and promoting the work of the Church. Through a greatly expanded Department of Publicity it kept the churches informed about needs and opportunities. The Council encouraged greater emphasis on stewardship and promoted the Every Member Canvass, Every Church Canvass, and Pre-Budget Canvass. Per-capita giving increased from $31.27 in 1930 to $95.00 in 1958, and gifts for benevolence work showed a fivefold gain in that period. Developing organization brought a greatly increased number of synod and presbytery executives. Local churches, enjoying large attendance and growing membership, turned more and more to the use of the rotary system in electing elders and deacons. In many of the large churches use was made of a multiple ministry, in addition to business managers, recreational leaders, etc.

This new vitality was matched by evidence of remarkable change. The spirit that was abroad in the Church in 1900 or even 1925 was no longer the same. Change was due to the fact that viewpoints which had been held by some in the Church now received the support of a majority of ministers and members. One area where change was apparent was that of the spirituality of the Church. There was no repudiation of the historic emphasis on the spiritual nature and function of the Church, but a growing social consciousness was evident. The years of depression had a noticeable influence. Experiences of those years led to many articles in church papers on economic and other injustices and on the role of the Church in helping to find remedies. The Synod of Virginia was in the vanguard of the movement asking for action. In the 1934 Assembly a Permanent Committee on Social and Moral Welfare was set up and directed to report "a program of scope and attitude for our Church."

While declaring its loyalty to the historic Southern Presbyterian position, the committee affirmed the duty of the Church to "present Christ's ideal for the individual and society" and "establish His Lordship . . . over every area of human life"; it "cannot remain indifferent to [political and economic] areas of life," and it must deal "with those actual evils in the individual life, and in the social order."[2] The Church had always recognized its duty to speak out on "moral and social problems that affect the progress of God's Kingdom," and had in the past made deliverances on mob rule, lynching, etc. The new departure was in the emphatic official declaration of responsibility for preaching the gospel not only to the individual but also to society, setting up a committee to gather data on the basis of which the Assembly could take action, and in the amount of attention devoted to social and moral problems.

The new development was not unchallenged. There was much opposition. Were not these issues controversial? Was this not a repudiation of the spiritual function of the Church? So argued many who sought to have the committee abolished. But the committee was continued and, with increasing prestige, led the Church in studies of marriage and divorce, neighborliness in race relations and economics, etc. The growing importance of the Church's message on social and moral issues was reflected in the creation in 1946 of a Department of Christian Relations with a full-time director. Its duties were to speak to the churches, to speak for them when commissioned to do so, to speak in its own name, and to carry on education.

This department, later made a Division of the Board of Church Extension, presented some notable documents to the Assembly, such as "States Rights and Human Rights" in 1949. When in 1954 racial integration was a burning issue, the department, in "The Church and Segregation," declared, "The General Assembly affirms that enforced segregation of the races is discrimination which is not in harmony with Christian theology and ethics, and that the Church, in its relationships to cultural patterns, should lead rather than follow."[3] In that same year "A Statement to Southern Christians" affirmed, "Having in mind the recent decision of the Supreme Court of the United States concerning segregation, the Assembly commends the principle of the decision and urges all members of our churches to consider thoughtfully and prayerfully the complete solution of the problem involved. It also urges all our people to lend their assistance to those charged with the duty of implementing the decision, and to remember that appeals to racial prejudice will not help but hinder the accomplishment of this aim."[4] Other steps were taken in subsequent years to provide that what the Assembly approved in the way of deliverances in the field of social and moral welfare would be worked into teaching materials of the Church.

Change was also evident in theological outlook, though the Church remained conservative. The 1939 Assembly, in interpreting a part of the ordination vow, declared that "the acceptance of the infallible truth and divine authority of the Scriptures, and of Christ as very and eternal God who became man by being born of a virgin, who offered Himself as a sacrifice to satisfy divine justice and reconcile us to God, who rose from the dead with the same body with which He suffered and who will return again to judge the world," is involved in that vow. Nevertheless, there was more liberty, a greater spirit of inquiry, and increased sensitivity to contemporary thought.

The findings of Biblical scholarship were more and more accepted and used in all of the seminaries. Belief in the multiple authorship of Isaiah or in the presence of various accounts in Genesis no longer endangered a ministerial candidate's ordination. Attempts to secure action against two well-known ministers on the basis of unsoundness of views failed when the views were not found contrary to the "system of doctrine." In 1944 Dispensationalism was declared out of accord with the Church's doctrine, and many presbyteries made special efforts to prevent the admission of any minister holding Dispensational views. Concern for the Church and loyalty to the program of the Southern Church were increasingly emphasized. A significant part of the changing theological climate was the evidence of a new theological creativity. Help was found in the insights of contemporary theologians in arriving at a new understanding of Reformation theology.

GREATER PARTICIPATION IN THE
ECUMENICAL MOVEMENT

The changing climate was shown in a new enthusiasm for the "ecumenical movement." Dissatisfaction with deliverances on social problems had led the Church to withdraw from the Federal Council of the Churches of Christ in America in 1931. Various Assemblies refused to re-enter the Council, and this position was supported by the presbyteries in 1937. But in 1941 the invitation to re-enter the Council was accepted. The Church shared in the formation of the National Council of the Churches of Christ in the United States of America in 1950. Boards of the Church participated in and supported the various departments of the Council and received aid from its interdenominational services and fellowship. There was unbroken participation in the great ecumenical conferences of the International Missionary Council, Faith and Order Movement, and Life and Work Movement. Membership in the World Council of Churches was accepted at the time of its formation.

In the field of ecumenical activities the great issue was a possible union with the Presbyterian Church in the United States of America, still referred to as the Northern Church. Interest in Christian unity, manifested also in other denominations at this time, was reflected in the maintenance for several years of a committee "On Union with All Other Presbyterian Bodies in the United States." In 1937 a Permanent Committee on Co-operation and Union was erected to "explore the possibilities of co-operation and union with other Presbyterian bodies." The initiative of this Southern Presbyterian committee led to negotiations with the Northern Church and later with the United Presbyterian Church. A detailed plan of union was drawn up, approved by the Assemblies of the three Churches, and in 1954 submitted to the presbyteries.

In the Southern Church there was much discussion. The plan was debated in church papers, presbyteries, and local churches. A vast amount of literature was circulated. Opponents of union cited the dangers of being "swallowed up," of greater centralization, and of the threat to property rights. The "lower view of the office of elder," allowance of women elders, "lower per-capita giving," and the "liberalism" of the Northern Church were pointed out, as well as the danger of "splitting the Southern Church." Those in favor of union stressed the common heritage, advantages of united work, gains from being a national Church, the soundness of the plan, and the integrity of the other Churches, and denied the dangers cited by those opposing merger. While the other Churches approved the union and joined in forming the United Presbyterian Church in the United States of America, the plan was defeated by the presbyteries of the Southern Church by a vote of 43-42 (1 tie). Since a three-fourths majority of the presbyteries was needed for approval, union failed by a good margin. Nevertheless, for the first time negotiation with the Northern Church had reached the stage of producing a detailed plan, and the movement for union had shown far more strength than in any previous period.

DIFFERING VIEWPOINTS PRODUCE TENSION

The discussions of social and moral problems, theological issues, and ecumenical activities produced evidence of a wide divergence of viewpoints in the Church. There were those occupying "middle ground," with some to the right and some to the left. Each group was seeking to know what it meant to be the Church in mid-twentieth-century America and what was the role of the Southern Church. Differences of convictions caused increasing tensions and led to a report to the 1955 Assembly by the Division of Christian Relations on "Unity in the Church with Diversity." Five causes of disunity were discussed. There were differences regarding principles and methods of Biblical interpretation, in evaluations placed on specific theological doctrines, in opinions regarding the application of the gospel to complex life situations, in judgments about co-operative relationships with other Church bodies, and in the understanding of the essential characteristics of the Presbyterian form of government.

Tensions in the Church were reflected in independent church papers. *The Southern Presbyterian Journal* was established in 1942. Its purpose was to "wave the banners which our heroic fathers lifted in the name of God."[5] The editors saw in the Church as a whole doctrinal departures which the Southern Church had not escaped, with the result that the gospel was being diluted. They contended for acceptance of "the integrity of Scripture," which apparently included verbal inerrancy. The mission of the Church was viewed as "strictly spiritual," with no "meddling . . . in economic, political, social and racial matters, and affairs of State."[6] In contrast to this meddling in society the true role of the Church was viewed as preaching the gospel to individuals. On racial matters the magazine was conservative, and voiced opposition to "enforced integration." In co-operative relationships the *Journal* promoted "a union of kindred spirits" rather than organic union, and opposed the Federal (later National) Council and the plan of union with the Northern Church. Traditional statements of doctrine were viewed as the best.

The Presbyterian Outlook, a descendant of Presbyterian newspapers in the South whose history extended back over a century, represented a different point of view. It promoted the union movement and the activities of the National Council. It sought to keep the Church informed and active on social issues, and strongly supported the Supreme Court decision and Assembly deliverances on race. The *Outlook* favored the rephrasing of the essential truths of traditional doctrinal statements in terms currently used, and welcomed the findings of Biblical scholarship. Toward the end of the period it merged with *The Presbyterian Tribune* and thus served readers in the Northern and Southern Churches. *The Christian Observer,* widely read, avoided taking sides on controversial issues.

REDEDICATION TO EVANGELISM

In spite of the tensions, the work of the Churches was prosecuted with vigor. Never had the Southern Church experienced such a period of growth as that from 1940-1961. Much of the credit for the advance lay in the 1939 rededication to evangelism. "Witness" was stressed as the business of every church and of every Christian. Various effective methods of evangelism were promoted, and aid was given in the use of these methods by a full-time staff. In later years more attention was devoted to the formulation of a Reformed theology of evangelism that would undergird and guide the use of methods.

The number of new members added on profession of faith increased from 16,000 in 1938 to over 29,000 in 1958. Sunday school enrollment rose from 425,000 to 717,000, and communicant membership from 497,000 to 875,000. Hundreds of outpost Sunday schools and chapels were set up. An average of one new congregation was organized each week. Presbyterian Development Councils, assisted by a Department of Urban Church, promoted growth in expanding urban centers. Attempts were made to promote interest in industrial communities and to bring the Church to serve all classes of people in the South. Through a Department of Town and Country Church, rural churches were given new encouragement and were aided with formation of larger parishes, establishment of rising minimum salaries, and special institutes for training ministers. For new and old churches there were vast building projects. Hundreds of new sanctuaries, educational centers, and manses were constructed. Approximately one-fourth of the total income of the churches was devoted to building purposes. Guidance to local churches in these projects was offered through a Department of Church Architecture.

Opportunities offered by means of mass communications were not neglected. The Church created a Division of Radio and Television (now a Permanent Committee). It aided in the establishment of the Protestant Radio Center. The Protestant Hour, in which the Church shared, received notable recognition and reached almost two hundred radio stations in the South, while hundreds of local churches broadcasted their own programs. Beginnings were made in television.

A new determination marked the conduct of work among Negroes. Over $2,000,000 was raised to strengthen Stillman College and for the purchase of sites and erection of new churches. The number of Negro members almost doubled in five years. Growth was not unrelated to a new attitude manifested in the Church. The separate Negro synod was abolished. Negro ministers were members of Negro presbyteries or of other presbyteries where there was no discrimination. They were accepted for training in all of the Church's seminaries.

IMPROVING THE PROGRAM OF CHRISTIAN NURTURE AND TRAINING

Expansion was matched by development of educational work. Beginning in 1944 there was a restudy of the Church's program of teaching and nurture, followed in later years by research and discussion on the subject of teaching materials, looking "Toward a Curriculum for the Covenant Community—the Church." The number of Directors of Christian Education, most of whom were graduates of the General Assembly's Training School (now the Presbyterian School of Christian Education), grew "by leaps and bounds" in local churches, presbyteries, and synods. Adult training was carried on through two thousand Men of the Church groups and three thousand Women of the Church groups, and through Sunday school classes. A ministry to college students was maintained on over two hundred campuses where local Westminster Fellowships were centers for training in the Christian life and in the meaning of the Christian faith. Faculty Christian Fellowships spread over the Church. For Junior High and Senior High young people, programs and organizations included new developments in camps and conferences and guidance in Christian vocation. To aid in the nurture of children, emphasis was given to the training of teachers, including the use of laboratory schools. Family education was promoted, with helps for family worship, family camping, etc. A part of the educational work was keeping church members informed on what the Church was doing. *The Presbyterian Survey*, enlarged and improved, became an example of good religious journalism and enjoyed a rapid rise in circulation. In addition to training, the Church provided care for some groups. A Division of Homes and Christian Welfare was established for a more effective ministry in children's homes, nursing homes, and homes for the aging.

Nowhere was advance needed more than in the fifteen senior colleges, including two with an affiliated relationship, and the seven junior colleges maintained by the Church at the close of the war. During the period Stillman Institute became an accredited senior college, a new institution was established in Florida, and in North Carolina a consolidation program was undertaken to ensure a strong school on a new campus. Enrollment in the Church's colleges, including a few Negroes in two institutions formerly restricted to white students, greatly increased. New buildings, improved curricula, and greater endowment were in evidence. Graduate scholarships provided by the Church aided in strengthening faculties.

The vitality and expansion of the Church were reflected in the seminaries. During depression years discussion of consolidation was revived but none took place. The wisdom of maintaining the separate institutions was revealed when at the close of the war enrollments rose rapidly and continued high. Entering students were given various psychological and aptitude tests to aid in better self-understanding. Pastoral counseling, Biblical theology, and Christian ethics were added as new areas of study. Field work was closely supervised as a part of the teaching program. An increasing emphasis on continuing education, fellowships, and lectureships made these institutions more and more the intellectual centers of the Church's life for the leaders in their respective areas. Visiting professors and foreign students helped maintain awareness of the World Church. Much of the credit for these stronger institutions, as well as stronger colleges, was due to surveys, at times involving all of them and at times only single institutions, revealing weaknesses and needed improvements. The seminaries shared in a nationwide restudy of theological education, much of the initiative for which came from the Southern Church.

CARRYING ON THE WORLD MISSION

The work of the Church abroad had to be undertaken with new vigor after the war. For fifteen years it had been disrupted and reduced by the depression and the international situation. The number of missionaries had decreased from 517 in 1924 to 328 in 1944. Since few new missionaries had been sent out, the missionary force on the fields was of a high average age. Budgets had been reduced over 50% and had never regained the 1930 level. Work in the Far East had known no peace since 1938. The fields there were completely evacuated during World War II and suffered extensive property destruction and damage. The problem, beginning in 1945, was the recruiting of sufficient missionaries to carry on an enlarged program. Four hundred and seventy-three new missionaries were sent to the field in thirteen years. By 1957 the total number of missionaries had grown to five hundred. While all missionaries had to be withdrawn from China, with the seizure of that country by the Communists, the missionary force in Africa and Brazil was doubled, and it was greatly strengthened in Japan and Mexico. Increased budgets made possible great expansion in medical, educational, and agricultural work, as well as in evangelistic outreach. While the cause of World Missions no longer received as large a proportion of Assembly's benevolences as formerly, appropriations for the cause continued to increase, reaching over $3,500,000 in 1958.

During the time of rebuilding, the fruits of the past labors of the Church were in evidence. Strong national Churches existed in Japan, Korea, Mexico, and Brazil, as well as in Taiwan, where the Southern Church had begun to aid work established by English and Canadian Presbyterians. A synod and nine presbyteries had been established in the Belgian Congo. Much of the leadership for these national Churches was being trained in strong colleges maintained by the Southern Church in some of the countries. New fields were entered in co-operation with other Churches. The Southern Church joined with the Presbyterian Church in the United States of America (now the United Presbyterian Church in the U.S.A.), the Evangelical and Reformed Church (now the United Church of Christ), and the Evangelical United Brethren in establishing work in Ecuador; with the Presbyterian Church of Brazil and the Presbyterian Church in the United States of America in work in Portugal; and joined with the Presbyterian Church in the United States of America, the Evangelical and Reformed Church, and the Reformed Church in supporting a mission in Iraq, established in 1924. This co-operative work was in addition to sharing in the enterprises of the Foreign Mission Division of the National Council of Churches and in those of the International Missionary Council.

The growth of autonomous independent Churches raised questions, faced by all Mission Boards, of Church-Mission relationships. In the "new day" in missions, some boards placed all missionaries under the National Church. The Southern Board adopted no single policy. Affirming the belief that the guidance of the Holy Spirit comes through the national Churches as well as through the Southern Church, it had sought when the issue arose to work out, in co-operation with national Church leaders, what appeared to be the best solution. On the basis of past experience, encouragement was not given to merging of mission and national Church, lest autonomy and self-support be undermined, but was given to the co-operation of mission and Church through co-ordinate committees. This was carried out especially in Brazil, and also in Taiwan and Korea where integration of mission and national Church had been suggested for a time by the General Assembly of the national Churches in those two countries. The new emphasis of missionary conferences on "partnership," while accepted, was thus implemented in a pattern of organization that the Southern Church had favored for several decades.

Not all the Church's work abroad was "mission" work. Some

of it consisted of aid in lands where Southern Presbyterian missionaries did not labor. Help was extended to areas of human need around the world. By co-operating with and sharing in the work of Church World Service and the World Council of Churches, the Southern Church provided relief and rehabilitation for hungry and suffering people. In addition the Church gave "Inter-Church" aid to assist Churches of the Reformed tradition in Europe.

This period, which began in the despair of 1930, proved the most significant period that the Southern Church had known. More than ever before it showed a determination to discover and serve the whole South. At the same time it did not forget its world mission. With new vigor it sought to apply the gospel to all of life. It received from and contributed to other Churches as it shared to a greater extent in the ecumenical movement. And it showed itself willing to think prayerfully and seriously of what it means to be the Church in the modern world.

CHAPTER VIII

Conclusion: Heritage and Mission

SOUTHERN PRESBYTERIANS have been history-conscious.
The great days of the past have not been forgotten, nor have
they been permitted to pass unnoticed. In 1866, 1911, and
1936 there were observances marking the anniversary of the organization in 1861 of the Southern Church as a distinct denomination. The approach of 1961 led to plans for a celebration. While
there was to be a "Centennial" occasion, it was to be placed in
a larger context. The year 1961 marked the completion of four
hundred years since Presbyterians from France landed on the
shores of Southern colonies in 1562. Almost three hundred years
had passed since Presbyterianism in the South began, about 1687,
an existence which had been uninterrupted. Emphasis was to be
on four centuries of "Heritage" and on opportunities and responsibilities of "Mission." Goals were participation with the United
Presbyterian Church in the United States of America in a great
evangelistic effort, "The Presbyterian Mission to the Nation,"
and contributions to aid Churches of the Reformed family around
the world. The observance became one of a series in the family of
Reformed Churches—the four hundredth anniversary of the
definitive edition of Calvin's *Institutes,* the centennial of the
Presbyterian Church of Brazil, etc.

"Heritage" was owned with gratitude. God's mercy and grace
had been poured out on "this plot in Christ's vineyard." This
part of His people had been used to lift up "the Crown Rights of
the Redeemer," and to bear witness to the spiritual nature and
function of the Church. That spiritual function, at times vari-
ously conceived, was increasingly seen to include a vocation of
witness in all areas of life.

The Southern Church had never thought of itself as the whole
of Christ's Church. While it experienced times when many of

125

its members did not stress participation with other parts of the Body of Christ and with other Churches of the Reformed family, a sense of sharing in and concern for the whole Church triumphed in a life of contributing to and receiving from the world-wide Christian community.

The Church was located in the southern part of the United States. A sense of the whole South and a sense of mission to all the people of the South had not always been strong. Concern for the Scotch-Irish and for the middle class of that people dominated periods in the history of Southern Presbyterians. God's mercy was manifested in an increasing victory over race and class and a growing ministry to the whole population.

Interest in foreign missions had long been expressed. This interest was strengthened in a discovery of and dedication to the world mission of the Church at home and abroad.

The Southern Church kept its conservatism in doctrine. "Purity of the gospel" remained a chief concern. This concern developed and matured until the stimulus of Christian scholars of various outlook was welcomed and Southern Presbyterians joined in rethinking the meaning of Christian faith in the world of today.

Southern Presbyterians, like other Churches of the Reformed family, were zealous for education. They had come not only to maintain schools and colleges and seminaries but to give more and more the support essential to have institutions of high excellence. And through the years they had developed a program of nurture and training of the laymen for understanding the Christian faith and for participation in Christian service.

While "Heritage" was owned and appreciated, it was not an end in itself, but was for "Mission." The strength gained in the past was the platform for Mission in the South, in the nation, and in the world.

CHART OF THE DIVISIONS AND REUNIONS IN MAINSTREAM AMERICAN PRESBYTERIANISM IN 18TH AND 19TH CENTURIES

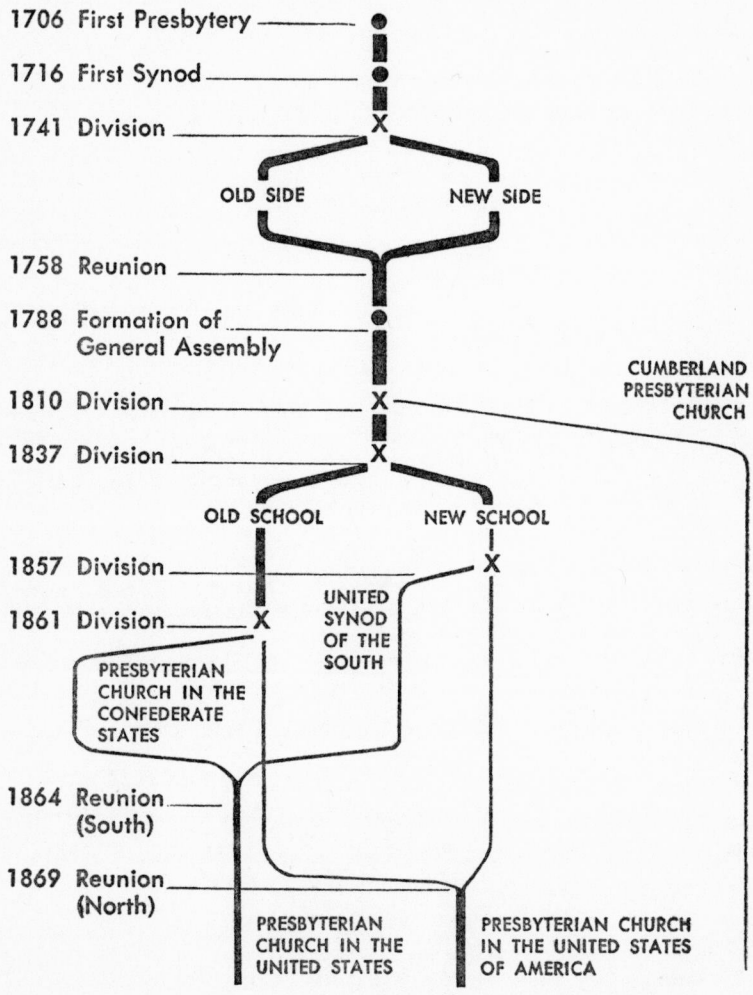

1706 First Presbytery

1716 First Synod

1741 Division

OLD SIDE   NEW SIDE

1758 Reunion

1788 Formation of General Assembly

CUMBERLAND PRESBYTERIAN CHURCH

1810 Division

1837 Division

OLD SCHOOL   NEW SCHOOL

1857 Division

1861 Division

UNITED SYNOD OF THE SOUTH

PRESBYTERIAN CHURCH IN THE CONFEDERATE STATES

1864 Reunion (South)

1869 Reunion (North)

PRESBYTERIAN CHURCH IN THE UNITED STATES

PRESBYTERIAN CHURCH IN THE UNITED STATES OF AMERICA

Bibliography

HISTORY OF THE CHRISTIAN CHURCH

Bainton, Roland H., *The Church of Our Fathers*. New York: Charles Scribner's Sons, 1941. (Revised edition.)

Latourette, Kenneth S., *A History of Christianity*. New York: Harper & Brothers, 1953.

THE CHURCH IN AMERICA

Brauer, Jerald C., *Protestantism in America*. Philadelphia: The Westminster Press, 1953.

Osborn, Ronald E., *The Spirit of American Christianity*. New York: Harper & Brothers, 1958.

Sweet, William W., *The Story of Religion in America*. New York: Harper & Brothers, 1950.

WORLD-WIDE PRESBYTERIANISM

Lingle, Walter L., *Presbyterians, Their History and Beliefs*. Richmond: John Knox Press, 1944, revised 1956.

Moffatt, James, *The Presbyterian Churches*. London: Methuen & Co., 1928.

Reed, R. C., *History of the Presbyterian Churches of the World*. Philadelphia: The Westminster Press, 1905. (Out of print.)

AMERICAN PRESBYTERIANISM

Armstrong, Maurice W., Loetscher, Lefferts A., Anderson, Charles A., editors, *The Presbyterian Enterprise: Sources of American Presbyterian History*. Philadelphia: The Westminster Press, 1956.

Slosser, Gaius J., editor, *They Seek a Country: The American Presbyterians, Some Aspects*. New York: The Macmillan Company, 1955.

Thompson, Robert E., *A History of the Presbyterian Churches in the U. S.*, American Church History Series, Vol. VI. New York: Charles Scribner's Sons, 1895. (Out of print.)

Trinterud, Leonard J., *The Forming of an American Tradition: A Re-examination of Colonial Presbyterianism*. Philadelphia: The Westminster Press, 1949.

Vander Velde, Lewis G., *The Presbyterian Churches and the Federal Union, 1861-1869*. Cambridge: Harvard University Press, 1932.

PRESBYTERIANISM IN THE SOUTH

Johnson, Thomas C., *History of the Southern Presbyterian Church*, American Church History Series, Vol. XI. New York: Charles Scribner's Sons, 1900. (Out of print.)

Posey, Walter B., *The Presbyterian Church in the Old Southwest, 1778-1838*. Richmond: John Knox Press, 1952.

Thompson, Ernest T., *Presbyterian Missions in the Southern United States.* Richmond: Presbyterian Committee of Publication, 1934. (Out of print.)

Thompson, Ernest T., *Tomorrow's Church/Tomorrow's World.* Richmond: John Knox Press, Fall 1960.

Wells, John M., *Southern Presbyterian Worthies.* Richmond: Presbyterian Committee of Publication, 1936. (Out of print.)

White, Henry A., *Southern Presbyterian Leaders.* The Neale Publishing Company, 1911. (Out of print.)

Acknowledgments

CHAPTER I. The Mother Presbytery

1. William Henry Foote, *Sketches of Virginia, Historical and Biographical,* p. 107. Philadelphia: W. S. Martien, 1849.
2. *Ibid.,* p. 128.
3. *Ibid.,* p. 163.
4. *Ibid.,* p. 193.
5. Albert Barnes, editor, *Sermons on Important Subjects by the Reverend Samuel Davies,* Vol. III, pp. 87-88, 226-227. New York: Robert Carter, 1854.
6. *Ibid.,* pp. 87-88.
7. Foote, *op. cit.,* p. 217.
8. Richard Webster, *A History of the Presbyterian Church in America, from Its Origin Until the Year 1760,* p. 558. Philadelphia: Presbyterian Historical Society, 1857.
9. Foote, *op. cit.,* p. 289.
10. *Ibid.,* p. 299.
11. Barnes, *op. cit.,* p. 499.
12. William Henry Foote, *Sketches of Virginia, Historical and Biographical,* Second Series, pp. 30-31. Philadelphia: J. B. Lippincott & Co., 1855.
13. Webster, *op. cit.,* p. 464.
14. *Ibid.*
15. George P. Hays, *Presbyterians, A Popular Narrative of Their Origin, Progress, Doctrines, and Achievements,* p. 480. New York: J. A. Hill & Company, 1892.
16. George Howe, *History of the Presbyterian Church in South Carolina,* Vol. I, p. 637. Columbia, S. C.: Duffie, Chapman, 1870.
17. Foote, *Sketches of Virginia,* Second Series, p. 360.
18. *Ibid.,* p. 56.
19. William Henry Foote, *Sketches of North Carolina, Historical and Biographical,* pp. 162, 167, 170, 165. New York: Robert Carter, 1846.
20. E. H. Gillett, *History of the Presbyterian Church in the United States of America,* revised, Vol. I, p. 425. Philadelphia: Presbyterian Board of Publication, 1864.
21. William B. Sprague, *Annals of the American Pulpit; or Commemorative Notices of Distinguished American Clergymen of Various Denominations,* Vol. III, p. 396. New York: Robert Carter & Brothers, 1856.
22. *Records of the Presbyterian Church in the United States of America,* p. 363. Philadelphia, 1841.
23. Foote, *Sketches of Virginia,* First Series, p. 324.
24. Foote, *Sketches of North Carolina,* p. 315.
25. *Journal of the Presbyterian Historical Society,* Vol. XII, No. 4, p. 196. Philadelphia: The Presbyterian Historical Society, 1927. Used by permission.

CHAPTER II. Growing Pains

1. *Records of the Presbyterian Church in the United States of America*, p. 525. Philadelphia, 1841.
2. Carter G. Woodson, *The History of the Negro Church*, pp. 84-85. Washington, D. C.: Associated Publishers, 1921.
3. Gillett, *History of the Presbyterian Church in the United States of America*, Vol. I, pp. 296-297.
4. *Minutes of the General Assembly of the Presbyterian Church in the United States of America*, 1789-1820, p. 91.
5. Gillett, *op. cit.*, Vol. I, p. 357.
6. *Minutes of the General Assembly*, 1789-1820, p. 238.
7. Gillett, *op. cit.*, Vol. I, p. 299.
8. Robert Davidson, *History of the Presbyterian Church in the State of Kentucky*, p. 138. New York: Robert Carter, 1847.
9. Robert Ellis Thompson, *A History of the Presbyterian Churches in the United States*, p. 71. New York: Charles Scribner's Sons, 1895.
10. Foote, *Sketches of Virginia*, Second Series, p. 437.
11. William Warren Sweet, *Religion on the American Frontier: The Presbyterians, 1783-1840*, pp. 763, 767. New York: Harper & Brothers, 1936. Used by permission.
12. Howe, *History of the Presbyterian Church in South Carolina*, Vol. II, p. 180.
13. *Ibid.*, p. 178.
14. Sweet, *op. cit.*, p. 783.
15. Sprague, *Annals of the American Pulpit*, Vol. IV, p. 591.
16. R. R. Gurley, *Life and Eloquence of the Rev. Sylvester Larned*, p. 61. New York: Wiley & Putnam, 1844.
17. T. M. Cunningham, *Hugh Wilson, A Pioneer Saint*, p. 110. Dallas: © T. M. Cunningham, 1938. Used by permission.
18. William M. Baker, *The Life and Labours of the Rev. Daniel Baker*, p. 158. Philadelphia: William S. & Alfred Martien, 1859.
19. Clifford Merril Drury, *Presbyterian Panorama*, p. 25. Philadelphia: Presbyterian Board of Christian Education, 1952. Used by permission.
20. Howe, *op. cit.*, Vol. II, p. 444.
21. *Minutes of the General Assembly of the Presbyterian Church in the United States of America*, 1789-1820, p. 427.
22. Foote, *Sketches of Virginia*, Second Series, p. 384.
23. William Maxwell, *A Memoir of the Rev. John H. Rice*, p. 3. Philadelphia: J. Whetham & Richmond Smith, 1835.
24. Sweet, *op. cit.*, p. 664.
25. William Childs Robinson, *Columbia Theological Seminary and the Southern Presbyterian Church*, p. 13. Decatur, Ga.: © William Childs Robinson, 1931. Used by permission.
26. *Memorial Volume of the Semi-Centennial of Columbia Theological Seminary*, p. 410. Columbia, S. C.: Presbyterian Publishing House, 1884.
27. Foote, *Sketches of Virginia*, Second Series, p. 304.
28. Gillett, *op. cit.*, Vol. II, p. 453.

29. Baker, *op. cit.*, pp. 205-206.
30. Thompson, *op. cit.*, pp. 107, 112.
31. *Ibid.*, p. 112.

CHAPTER III. "Our Southern Zion"

1. Peyton Harrison Hoge, *Moses Drury Hoge: Life and Letters,* p. 90. Richmond: Presbyterian Committee of Publication, 1899.
2. *Ibid.*, p. 101.
3. Robinson, *Columbia Theological Seminary and the Southern Presbyterian Church,* p. 32.
4. Thompson, *A History of the Presbyterian Churches in the United States,* pp. 369-370.
5. B. M. Palmer, *The Life and Letters of James Henley Thornwell,* p. 332. Richmond: Whittet & Shepperson, 1875.
6. John B. Adger and John L. Girardeau, editors, *The Collected Writings of James Henley Thornwell,* Vol. IV, p. 232. Richmond: Presbyterian Committee of Publication, 1872.
7. Thompson, *op. cit.*, p. 364.
8. *Ibid.*, p. 371.
9. Thomas Cary Johnson, *The Life and Letters of Benjamin Morgan Palmer,* p. 10. Richmond: Presbyterian Committee of Publication, 1906. Used by permission.
10. Palmer, *op. cit.*, pp. 477, 479.
11. Thomas Cary Johnson, *The Life and Letters of Robert Lewis Dabney,* p. 215. Richmond: Presbyterian Committee of Publication, 1903.
12. *Ibid.*, p. 224.
13. Johnson, *The Life and Letters of Benjamin Morgan Palmer,* pp. 213, 217.
14. *Minutes of the Synod of South Carolina,* 1860, p. 29.
15. Thompson, *op. cit.*, pp. 379-380.
16. *Southern Presbyterian* (Columbia, S. C.), July 6, 1861.
17. *Memorial Addresses Delivered Before the General Assembly of 1886* (Presbyterian Church, U.S.), p. 53.
18. Palmer, *op. cit.*, p. 493.
19. *Proceedings of a Convention of Delegates from Various Presbyteries in the Confederate States of America,* 1861, p. 13.

CHAPTER IV. The Presbyterian Church in the Confederate States

1. Adger and Girardeau, *The Collected Writings of James Henley Thornwell,* Vol. IV, pp. 465-466.
2. *Minutes of the General Assembly of the Confederate States of America* (first Confederate Assembly), 1861, Vol. I, pp. 7, 71-72, 51-60, 15-17, 12.
3. *Abstract of the Minutes of Harmony Presbytery,* March 1865, p. 52.
4. *Minutes of the Synod of North Carolina,* 1862, p. 17.
5. *Minutes of Harmony Presbytery,* March 1865, p. 52.
6. Johnson, *The Life and Letters of Benjamin Morgan Palmer,* pp. 278-279.
7. Hoge, *Moses Drury Hoge: Life and Letters,* pp. 150-151.
8. *Minutes of the General Assembly,* 1862, p. 35.
9. Johnson, *The Life and Letters of Robert Lewis Dabney,* p. 236.

10. William Sterling Lacy, *Memorial Addresses*, pp. 60-61. Richmond: Presbyterian Committee of Publication, 1900.
11. *Minutes of the Synod of Virginia*, 1863, p. 327.
12. *Minutes of the Presbytery of South Alabama*, in *Records of the Synod and Presbyteries of Alabama*, 1832-1866, p. 378.
13. R. Q. Mallard, *Plantation Life Before Emancipation*, p. 204. Richmond: © R. Q. Mallard, 1892.

CHAPTER V. Desolations Repaired

1. *Minutes of the Synod of Virginia*, 1865, p. 379.
2. *Minutes of Harmony Presbytery*, October 1866, p. 54.
3. *Minutes of the Synod of South Carolina*, 1865, p. 212.
4. *Minutes of the General Assembly*, 1865, pp. 383, 386, 388.
5. *Minutes of the General Assembly*, 1866, pp. 45, 44.
6. *Ibid.*, p. 49.
7. *Minutes of the General Assembly*, 1870, p. 521.
8. *The True Presbyterian*, June 19, 1862.
9. *Minutes of the Synod of Kentucky*, 1865, p. 24.
10. Thomas C. Johnson, *A History of the Southern Presbyterian Church*, p. 466, footnote. New York: The Christian Literature Co., 1894.
11. *Ibid.*, p. 454.
12. John S. Grasty, *Memoir of Rev. Samuel B. McPheeters, D.D.*, p. 200. St. Louis: Southwestern Book & Publishing Company, 1870.
13. *Minutes of the General Assembly*, 1865, pp. 382-389.
14. *Minutes of the General Assembly*, 1867, p. 145.
15. *Minutes of the General Assembly*, 1874, p. 517.
16. *Minutes of the General Assembly*, 1865, p. 396.
17. *Minutes of the General Assembly*, 1876, pp. 233-234.
18. Johnson, *The Life and Letters of Benjamin Morgan Palmer*, p. 478.
19. *Southern Presbyterian Review*, 1875, Vol. XXVI, pp. 665-668.
20. Hoge, *Moses Drury Hoge: Life and Letters*, pp. 284-286.
21. *Minutes of the General Assembly*, 1870, p. 516.
22. *Ibid.*, p. 517.
23. Johnson, *The Life and Letters of Robert Lewis Dabney*, p. 352.
24. *Minutes of the General Assembly*, 1870, pp. 542-543.
25. Johnson, *op. cit.*, p. 355.
26. *Minutes of the General Assembly*, 1875, pp. 96-100.
27. *Minutes of the General Assembly*, 1870, pp. 537 ff.
28. *Minutes of the General Assembly*, 1882, p. 531.
29. *Memorial Addresses Delivered Before the General Assembly of 1886*, pp. 54, 57.

CHAPTER VI. The Church in the New South

1. *Southern Presbyterian Review*, July 1885, Vol. XXXVI, p. 423.
2. *Ibid.*, p. 439.
3. Marion W. Woodrow, *Dr. James Woodrow, As Seen by His Friends*, p. 780. Columbia, S. C.: © Marion W. Woodrow, 1909. Used by permission.
4. *Ibid.*, p. 659.

5. *Minutes of the General Assembly*, 1888, p. 408.
6. Woodrow, *op. cit.*, p. 973.
7. John B. Adger, *My Life and Times, 1810-1899*, p. 462. Richmond: Presbyterian Committee of Publication, 1899.
8. *Minutes of the General Assembly*, 1906, p. 23.
9. *Minutes of the General Assembly*, 1880, p. 186.
10. *Minutes of the General Assembly*, 1891, p. 260.
11. *Minutes of the General Assembly*, 1916, p. 47.
12. Mary D. Irvine and Alice L. Eastwood, *Pioneer Women of the Presbyterian Church in the United States*, pp. 51-52. Richmond: Presbyterian Committee of Publication, 1923. Used by permission.
13. *Minutes of the General Assembly*, 1907, p. 101.
14. *Christian Observer*, December 11, 1901.
15. *Minutes of the General Assembly*, 1929, p. 80.
16. *Minutes of the General Assembly*, 1907, p. 50.
17. *Minutes of the General Assembly*, 1919, p. 55.
18. *Minutes of the General Assembly*, 1920, p. 74.

CHAPTER VII. Changing Climate

1. *Minutes of the General Assembly*, 1949, pp. 131, 162.
2. *Minutes of the General Assembly*, 1935, p. 93.
3. *Minutes of the General Assembly*, 1954, p. 193.
4. *Ibid.*, p. 197.
5. *Southern Presbyterian Journal*, May 1942, Vol. I, No. 1, p. 3.
6. *Ibid.*, p. 5.